WOMEN WITHOUT WALLS

MARY COTES

WOMEN WITHOUT WALLS

HOW GOD SHAPES ORDINARY WOMEN
FOR EXTRAORDINARY KINGDOM WORK

GRACEWORKS

Women Without Walls
Copyright © 2021 by Mary Cotes

All rights reserved. No part of this publication may be reproduced, stored in a retrieval system, or transmitted, in any form or by any means, electronic, mechanical, photocopying, recording or otherwise, without the prior written permission of the author, except in the case of brief quotations embodied in critical articles and reviews.

Published by Graceworks Private Limited
22 Sin Ming Lane
#04-76 Midview City
Singapore 573969
Tel: 67523403
Email: enquiries@graceworks.com.sg
Website: www.graceworks.com.sg

All Scripture quotations, unless otherwise noted, are taken from the New Revised Standard Version Bible, copyright © 1989 National Council of the Churches of Christ in the United States of America. Used by permission. All rights reserved worldwide.

Typefaces: Nocturne Serif, Alegreya Sans, Trajan Pro

ISBN: 978-981-14-7156-8

2 3 4 5 6 7 8 9 10 · 28 27 26 25 24 23 22 21

*This book is for Lifesprings International,
encouraging, preparing and connecting women worldwide
to impact their communities with the love of God,
for the bilingual school of ministry—Formation Zoé—
in Lyon, France.*

*The words of the Lord are like the yeast
when it first gets to work in the dough of our lives,
making it rise with a new way of life.*
Madeleine Delbrêl

Contents

The Kingdom Announced — 1

I. **Crossing Divides: The Open Kingdom** — 15
   The inclusivity of Jesus' ministry;
   Karla Faye Tucker (1959–1998): American prisoner
      on death row;
   St. Perpetua and St. Felicitas (third century):
      African martyrs

II. **Seeking Signs: The Mysterious Kingdom** — 40
   The women of the genealogy (Matt. 1:1–17): Tamar, Rahab,
      Ruth, Bathsheba and Mary.

III. **Serving Others: The Humble Kingdom** — 66
   Peter's mother-in-law (Matt. 8:14–15);
   Sabina Bell (1919–2015): English social worker

IV. **Reaching Out: The Welcoming Kingdom** — 86
   The woman with the flow of blood (Matt. 9:20–22);
   Dorcas Price (b.1917): Welsh night-shelter volunteer

V. **Staying True: The Enduring Kingdom** — 111
   The Canaanite woman (Matt. 15:21–28);
   Sojourner Truth (1797?–1883): African-American
      freed slave, preacher and abolitionist

VI. **Loving Action: The Powerful Kingdom** — 145
   The woman with the perfume (Matt. 26:6–13);
   Amy Carmichael (1867–1951): Irish missionary in India

VII. **Giving All: The Transformative Kingdom** — 171

The mother of James and John (Matt. 20:20–28; 27:55–56);
Alice Domon (1937–1977): French religious in Argentina,
active with the mothers of the disappeared

VIII. Living Hopefully: The Promised Kingdom   199
The two Marys at the empty tomb (Matt. 27:59–61; 28:1–10);
Betsie (1885–1944) and Corrie ten Boom (1892–1983): Dutch
rescuers, prisoners in Ravensbrück Nazi concentration camp

The Yeast in Our Lives: Ambassadors of the Kingdom Today *229*

Bibliography   *241*

Acknowledgements

This book could not have seen the light of day without the support and insight of many people. First I should like to thank my editor, Nicole Ong, for her brilliantly incisive comments and wise suggestions, all of which have made the final stages of writing this book a great pleasure. I would also like to express my gratitude to those who read the manuscript in its early stages, including Pauline Barnes, Marie-France Favier, Stephen Norrish, Graham Ghaleb, Geoff Colmer and my friends at St. James' Church, New Bradwell, who each offered valuable reactions and comments. I am indebted too to Revd. Dr. Phil Wall and Revd. Andrew McLaughlin, ministers in the Pontypridd area, for their wisdom in relation to Chapter IV. Thanks are due also to Jacqueline Oléart, Gladys Deleuze and Edith Grandjean, without whom the book would never have first been written in French, and to Kae Ting who has helped the book on its journey from French into English. Finally I would like to thank not only my husband Duncan for his unflinching support of me while I sat at the kitchen table and wrote this book, but also my mother Lorna, a woman without walls, who—despite evidence to the contrary—has always faithfully expressed her confidence in my abilities.

The Kingdom Announced

This is a book about the many ways in which God calls women to be ambassadors of his Kingdom. How does God prepare women to change the world around them? How can they be active players in the world as Christian disciples, to build communities shaped by the love, justice and peace that are so central to God's purposes? These are the pressing questions that lie at the heart of what follows.

This is not a book about how women can become good Christian wives and mothers. It offers no special advice on how to bring up children or grandchildren, or how to be devoted in marriage. Down the years there have been many wise and expert authors who have written on these subjects. However, this author is not adding her name to the list! Instead, the starting point of what is written here is the profound conviction that the Gospels present women not principally as wives and mothers and grandmothers, but ultimately as passionate followers of Christ. They are called to be faithful to the values of the Kingdom of God in every aspect of their daily lives.

The Kingdoms of this World and the Kingdom of God

The inspiration for this book goes back to the morning of 15 July 2016, when I received an email from a French friend whose daughter lives in Nice. The previous evening, a devastating terrorist attack had taken place in the city and my friend's young granddaughter had thought that she had heard one of her school friends named amongst those dead. An icy fear rose inside me. Yet another terrible event. In the months before, there had been terrorist attacks in Charleston, Paris and Brussels. Then in June, Jo Cox, one of our British MPs, had been murdered just a few days before the 'Brexit' vote. Since the day of that referendum, our Polish friends who live on the other side of the city had been spat upon as they got on a bus. One of our French church members had been insulted by his British colleagues on his arrival at work. An Italian neighbour had been punched by a man she had politely greeted on arrival at the gym. A strange and pernicious force seemed to have been let loose and everything seemed to be veering out of control. What was becoming of us? I was overwhelmed by a crushing sense of apprehension, not just for my own nation and our social and political relationships, but for the stability of the whole world currently so torn by fear and hatred, poverty and war.

I was sitting at my desk and began to leaf through the pages of the Gospels. I was both comforted and challenged to discover once again that Jesus also lived in a world that was poisoned by political turmoil and racial tension. Fear dominated everyday life. The Roman occupation of Palestine had been in existence for some hundred years and there seemed to be no end to it in sight. Far from bringing the promised peace of the 'pax romana', the occupation brought the threat of violence that could explode at any moment. The Roman army was present everywhere; behind every centurion who appears in the Gospels there were a hundred Roman soldiers. This Roman 'kingdom' exercised an iron grip on the population and imposed a crippling system of unjust and exorbitant taxation. Those who refused to pay and those who were unable to do so were heavily punished, tortured or put to death. Crucifixion, the death penalty imposed by the Romans, was intended to serve as a discouragement to trouble-makers.

This state of affairs provoked different reactions amongst

different groups. Certain Jews—of which Herod was one—collaborated with Roman power and lined their pockets at the same time. Other Jews looked back with a great sense of nostalgia to King David's empire and longed for the day when the power of the Roman occupation would be overthrown and a national 'kingdom' put in its place. Some plotted violent revolution.

Meanwhile, the empire attracted a large number of immigrant traders who lived in the non-Jewish areas of the region. Certain pious Jews were more fearful than ever that the number and influence of non-Jews in the area would destroy the integrity of the Jewish nation before God. Far from wanting to collaborate with the Romans, they dreamed of a different 'kingdom' built upon the religious and cultural purity of their people. They encouraged Jews to live separately from Gentiles and maintain the religious and cultural practices that defined their Jewish identity.

And the people in the middle found themselves the victims of distrust. If they hated the Romans for inflicting a military occupation, they also despised them for being Gentiles. The mistrust they felt in relation to the Romans poisoned their everyday relationships with their fellows. Who was a collaborator? Who belonged to the resistance? Who would exploit them and make money at their expense? In such a social climate, it was entirely understandable that anger, despair and hatred should seep into the minds and hearts of all the people. The whole of society was imbued by an atmosphere of toxic values that could quickly and effortlessly eradicate faith, hope and love.

As I reread the pages of the Gospel that morning of 15 July, I felt as if I was hearing the teaching of Jesus in a new way. In the midst of a scary, divided world not too different from our own, Jesus invites his followers to seek another Kingdom. Turning to his followers who are as tired of present realities as they are fearful for the future, he calls them to reject the pernicious values with which they are surrounded. Instead of recommending that they give vent to anger and distrust, or seek the expulsion of any and all who do not resemble them, Jesus calls them to, "...seek first the kingdom of God" (Matt. 6:33a, ESV).

The proclamation of the Kingdom of God is central to Jesus' ministry. He announces it right from the very moment when, at the start of the Gospel story, he comes into Galilee and calls his listeners, men and women alike, to seek a dramatic change in their lives: Repent! Be converted! Jesus speaks of a categorical change of orientation. Stop, turn around, and go in the opposite direction. He is not recommending a superficial lifestyle change or the violent replacement of one military power by another. Nor is he advocating the practice of a private, self-absorbed spirituality. Rather, he is pointing to a profound transformation that will begin within each one and *overflow into the whole of society*.

What an extraordinary invitation! If the disciples of Jesus have the impression that nothing can possibly change for the better, Jesus points to a new reality: the possibility of living according to God's values. All those who follow Jesus have the chance to leave behind a life lived according to the values of their contemporary context, and live according to the values of God. Jesus himself will manifest those values. To those who give expression to their own deepest fears by seeking to dominate others, Jesus shows the way of service. To those who seek to protect themselves either by separating themselves from people who are different or by pushing them away, he speaks of love. To those who are so tired and fearful that they want to give up trying, he offers the grace of God to persevere. The liberating values of the Kingdom are not like those of the kingdoms of this world. As the prophet Isaiah proclaimed centuries before,

*For my thoughts are not your thoughts,
nor are your ways my ways, says the Lord (Is. 55:8).*

The Challenge to Women

Side by side as faithful disciples of Christ, both men and women are called by God to make a difference in the world around them through the active testimony they offer in their daily lives. They are to be ambassadors of God's Kingdom. This invitation to all nonetheless often represents a particular challenge to women as it places a special calling upon them. As those who, down the centuries, have traditionally been associated with roles played out exclusively in the private sphere, the invitation to be disciples in the world can require a change of gear and mind-set. While recent decades have seen more and more women become powerful players in the public sphere, in person and online, many parts of the Church have persisted in defining women's role as one that is first and foremost engaged with the family. Yet women's Christian calling is not limited to, or defined by, their roles as wives or mothers. Just as women in Jesus' time responded to his revolutionary invitation to follow by journeying with him all the way from Galilee to Jerusalem, so today, women are called to step out of their hiding places. They are invited to play their full part as confident heralds of the Kingdom wherever God has placed them.

Christ's call to his followers to be entrepreneurs for God's Kingdom, living fully as disciples of Christ in the world, can also come as a shock to women who have often been taught to think that 'real' Christian women must be demure and reticent, not to say passive. For centuries, churchgoers were instructed to believe that a virtuous woman in God's sight was a silent woman, and these instructions have seeped deep into our Christian DNA. Only now are women beginning to find their voice and speak truthfully in public. For many, it still remains a huge challenge to do so. Yet Christ's call to full discipleship invites women to break free from the expectations with which tradition has often burdened them, and to reject the labels that have impeded their full and confident growth into the image of Christ.

Women who follow Jesus Christ are not called to stay trembling in the wings, for fear of being thought by the Church to be 'unwomanly' or 'unchristian'. As they respond to Christ's call, which is offered to men and women alike, they become full citizens of the Kingdom of God, allowing God to transform society through them. Even if this challenge to women may often have been side-lined by elements of the Christian Church in the past, it has always been ringing out loud and clear from the Scriptures. In this book, we ask what kind of spiritual journey women need to embark on, to respond to it anew for our own times.

Inspiration from Women Who Have Gone Before Us

Down the centuries, preachers and writers have recounted wonderful stories about great men of God, and often omitted to tell the equally wonderful stories about great women. These latter stories lay largely forgotten to many parts of the Christian Church and have only recently started to re-emerge. This has inevitably led to a situation in which the Church has not quickly or easily understood women as agents of the Kingdom with substantial gifts to offer in Christian witness and mission.

If women are to play their full part as witnesses to God's Kingdom in the world, they need the encouragement offered by the testimonies of women who have gone before. They need to know by heart the remarkable stories of their indomitable Spirit-filled courage and gritty determination. Women, as well as men, are bearers of God's image and faithful imitators of Christ.

Gospel Women

In view of this, this book reflects unashamedly on the stories of the ordinary women made extraordinary who appear in the Gospel of Matthew. Each chapter offers a focus on one of these inspirational figures. As those who encountered Jesus, each one has a special story to tell; each one, in her own way, becomes an ambassador for the Kingdom of God. Some of them, like the Canaanite woman or the woman with the perfume, were only in Jesus' company for a matter of minutes or hours. Others, like the mother of James and John or Mary of Magdala, were in his company for a much longer time, perhaps a number of years. But whatever the length of the meeting, each one was transformed in one way or another by her encounter with Christ, and became a herald of the Kingdom. What might these Biblical women have to teach women today, as the Church grapples with the challenge of offering Christian witness in this divided world?

Women from Different Times

Yet these Biblical women do not appear in this book on their own. Their stories are accompanied by parallel testimonies of courageous, visionary and feisty women of God from other times in Christian history. From the first centuries, we come across Perpetua and her slave Felicitas. We encounter Julian of Norwich from medieval times, and Teresa of Avila from the sixteenth century. From the seventeenth century, there is Margaret Fell, and from the eighteenth and nineteenth centuries, we shall look at the testimonies of Sojourner Truth and Amy Carmichael to name but two. From modern times, we meet, amongst others, Alice Domon and Karla Faye Tucker. The presence of these women in this book is an indication that the call to women to be active, faithful disciples in the world is not simply a product of modern thinking. God has *always* been calling women into the service of Christ and inviting them to play their full part as builders of Kingdom community, and women of faith have *always* been responding. As those called to be faithful today, we must raise the visibility of these our Christian sisters from other times and other places and be inspired and encouraged by their stories. In their turn, Christian women today need to learn the importance of telling their own stories of faith in their own voices in order to encourage those who come after them to live faithfully in their own times.

... From Different Places

The women included in the chapters that follow come also from a range of different countries. Amongst the women whom we look at from Matthew's Gospel, there are Jews and Canaanites, not to mention a Moabite and a Hittite. Amongst other witnesses quoted in this book, there are women from Europe, from Asia and Russia, not to mention the Americas and Africa. Standing alongside each other, these bold women of God remind us of the critically significant role that women have to play wherever they may find themselves in the international community of faith. Although culture plays an important part in shaping expectations and possibilities for action, the call itself to be an active player for the Kingdom of God is not ultimately dependent on the particular culture to which a woman belongs. In every place women are called by God to be unafraid, and to incarnate the values of the Kingdom for their own cultural context.

... With Different Family Circumstances

A range of different family circumstances are represented by the stories told here. Of the women included in this book, some are married or widowed, like the mother of James and John, Catherine Booth and Sabina Bell. Others are unmarried, such as Amy Carmichael and Alice Domon. Others again are divorced, such as Sojourner Truth who, once freed from slavery, parted from the man she had been forced to marry. Some have children, some do not. Whatever their marital status, these women remind us that God's principal calling upon women is to be faithful as disciples. After all, in the Gospels, Jesus never commanded anyone to go and get married or to go and have children. He called them to follow him.

... Shaped by Different Christian Traditions

The women we discuss in this book also represent a wide range of different Christian traditions. Sojourner Truth's powerful conversion experience came at the time she was living with the Wageners—a Quaker couple who had shared their faith with her. After leaving their home, she worshipped in a Methodist church. The evangelical Corrie ten Boom came from a Dutch Reformed Church background, while Mary Skobtsova, imprisoned also in Ravensbrück for having assisted Jews, was from the Russian Orthodox tradition. Sabina Bell came from an evangelical family, Alice Domon was a Roman Catholic, and Amy Carmichael, who was brought up in a Presbyterian home, ended up incorporating an eclectic selection of worship-styles into the services held in the community in India that she founded.

The history of the divisions that have torn the Church apart down through the centuries does not make for very uplifting reading! As those who have inherited the divisions, we still suffer from the wounds inflicted by them. The women we discuss in this book worshipped in very different ways one from another and undoubtedly had very divergent views on many aspects of Christian faith and doctrine. However, each one of them, in relation to Christ, held passionately to a vision of the Kingdom that shaped her life. Each one longed to see the Kingdom become a reality and did not wait to set to work in the place where God had placed her. These women are placed alongside one another in this book as a sign that in his great goodness, God does not limit himself to inviting into his service only Evangelicals or only Catholics. Christ calls one and all, however different from one another we may be, to witness with faith and perseverance to his Kingdom in every corner of the world, even in the most distant and the most challenging of places.

... Surrounded by Other Witnesses

While this book presents the story of one woman of modern times in each chapter, it is also vitally important to remember that not one of them would have had the ministry she did without the support of others: family members, friends, colleagues and other Christians. Men and women of faith stand beside and behind each one. Hidden by the brevity of the biographies offered here, they nonetheless played a vital role in the witness of these women to the Gospel. Sojourner Truth never ceased to be grateful to the couple who had bought her freedom, while Corrie ten Boom expresses her gratitude, throughout her books, both to the upbringing and wisdom she received from her father and from the inspiration she drew from the spirituality of her sister. Alice Domon was supported by her colleagues and friends, by priests and parishioners who welcomed her, and by the Mothers of the Plaza de Mayo alongside whom she worked. Meanwhile, Sabina Bell was supported by her husband in the same way as she supported him. Their lives stand as a reminder that women are not only to be supporters of others, both men and women, but also to be supported by others, both men and women. They lead us also to give thanks for the gift and dramatically inclusive nature of the Christian community into which God calls us.

A Call to All Women

The names of a handful of the women in this book, such as Betsie and Corrie ten Boom, will probably be well-known to many readers. Other names will be known to only a few. Others again will be wholly unknown to all except those who knew them personally and to the author herself. They are presented here alongside one another, in deliberate defiance of the current cult of celebrity that often blinds us to the essential truth of the Gospel: each and every one of us is special to God and has an essential role to play in the life of the Kingdom. This can be a special challenge to those women who have assumed without question that those whose efforts 'count' most in the mission of God's Kingdom must be the great men. The call to follow Christ faithfully in the world is not just offered to the famous, extraordinary few or to women who are specially singled out, but to each and every one.

The Parable of the Yeast

As a teacher, Jesus never wrote theological treaties or used heavy theological language. Rather, he spoke of deep spiritual realities through the simple language of parables. The Kingdom of God "is like this", Jesus often said: like the sower who goes out to sow, like the mustard seed, or the pearl of great value, or the treasure hidden in a field, or like the yeast that leavens the whole dough. Just as the surfaces of a diamond each reflect the light differently, so each parable offers a myriad of different truths around the theme. Those who seek the Kingdom of God are invited to reflect on these parables, trusting that the divine values they express have the power to transform our individual lives and of those around us.

The one Biblical woman who accompanies us through each chapter in this book is the baker of Jesus' parable of the yeast. On the surface, the parable appears to offer a gentle, domestic image, but underneath it is bursting with hope, energy and the promise of dynamic transformation. Throughout this book, we shall be using this extraordinary parable as a lens through which to reflect on the nature of God's Kingdom and the way in which women become its ambassadors.

> *He told them another parable: "The kingdom of heaven is like yeast that a woman took and mixed in with three measures of flour until all of it was leavened." (Matt. 13:33)*

At the time of Jesus, the huge range of work that women did was very largely invisible. What in those days was thought of as 'proper' work—business management, crafting, building and selling, judging and writing—went on in the public sphere. This was generally considered to be a male-dominated space to which women did not belong. According to the thinking of the ancient world, women belonged to the private sphere, which was the hidden world of the home. Of course, they still did plenty of work in the home, including grinding the flour and baking the bread. It is quite clear that women were far from idle; their work was simply not recognised or valued as such. And while men—such as Matthew the *tax-collector* or Simon-Peter and Andrew the *fishermen*—were often defined according to the work they did in the public sphere, women—such as Mary *the mother of Joses*—were not defined by their activities but according to the relationships they had instead. More rarely, like Mary *of Magdala*, they were defined according to where they came from.

For all its brevity, the significance of the parable of the yeast grows deeper when seen against this cultural backdrop. In telling it, Jesus puts a woman centre-stage and makes her activity visible. In the same way, he makes women visible throughout the course of his ministry and calls them into full and active discipleship. What is more, in describing the way in which the baker kneads enough dough to satisfy an enormous crowd of hungry people, Jesus offers a powerful image of the way God is at work in the world, mixing the abundant life of the Kingdom into its furthest and most forgotten corners. This parable has the power to change the way we think, act and speak.

The world in which we live as Christ's disciples today has, arguably, always been a dangerous place, torn apart by fears and hatreds of every kind. However, the world does not seem to be getting any safer, fairer or more peaceful. Quite the opposite. As Jesus predicted, the poor are still with us. In recent years, we have seen violence continuing to rear its ugly head, threatening not only human communities, but also the very sustainability of God's creation. Continuing violence done to women forms a highly significant part of this devastating picture.

The language of division, of them-and-us, has become a commonplace in public discourse, both online and offline, while the recent coronavirus pandemic has served to highlight and exacerbate tensions and divisions between nations. This is not a time for the Christian Church to hide away in a cocoon of private or fearful spirituality. We are called to be followers of Christ not just within the community of the church or in the home, but in the world around us. The life of the Kingdom of God is not a reality reserved only for the Christian community or for the family life of Christians. But, in Christ, it is offered to the whole of creation. What kind of Kingdom spirituality shall women need to equip them to fulfil this calling? As we reflect on the parable in the following chapters, we ask how we might live more faithfully as children of God and disciples of Christ, and how the yeast of the Kingdom might be active in every aspect of our daily lives.

1 Crossing Divides: The Open Kingdom

If we are to better the future we must disturb the present.
Catherine Booth[1]

If we have no peace, it is because we have forgotten that we belong to each other.
Mother Teresa of Calcutta[2]

I have a colleague who is almost obsessively passionate about making bread. She never stops talking about her most recent successes. She spends her days off experimenting with different recipes for wholemeal and devotes entire holidays to going on bread-making courses run by various famous bread chefs. One day, at the end of a meeting, she invited us all to stay on to watch her preparing her dough. She laid the ingredients out on the kitchen surface and went to work in front of us, explaining the various different stages of the process as she went. Excitement was written all over her face. I was captivated by the steely focus with which she set about the task, and the care she took over every detail. All the flour needed to be incorporated. She did not want to lose a single little bit.

---
1   (1829–1890), co-founder of the Salvation Army with her husband William.
2   (1910–1997), Albanian-Indian religious, school-teacher, headmistress and founder of the Missionaries of Charity.

As I watched my friend at work, I learnt something important about the commitment that goes into making bread. No part of the dough can be neglected. A baker knows that for the bread to come out of the oven big and beautifully risen, the yeast cannot be allowed to stay just at the centre of the mixture. It has to be worked on equally throughout so that it can reach every corner of the mixture, even the flour at the very edges.

It is this same picture that lies at the heart of Jesus' extraordinary parable. Comparing the Kingdom of God to the way that yeast works, Jesus describes how the action of the yeast leavens not just a section of the dough, but the *whole* lump. By using this powerful image, Jesus reminds us that the Kingdom of God, just like the yeast, is alive and at work everywhere. Nowhere and no one is left out of God's purposes. There is no corner of the world from which God is entirely absent. No situation is so desperate that God has withdrawn from it. No place is too foreign or forgotten for the Kingdom of God to be at work there in all its mystery.

> *Where can I go from your spirit?*
>   *Or where can I flee from your presence?*
> *If I ascend to heaven, you are there;*
>   *if I make my bed in Sheol, you are there.*
> *If I take the wings of the morning*
>   *and settle at the farthest limits of the sea,*
> *even there your hand shall lead me,*
>   *and your right hand shall hold me fast*
> *(Ps. 139:7–10).*
>
> *Holy, holy, holy is the Lord of hosts:*
> *the whole earth is full of his glory (Is. 6:3).*

The Ministry of Jesus: A Kingdom without Boundaries

Everyone and Everywhere!

The Kingdom of God is not the property of a few chosen people, but is offered to the whole world. Even the most superficial reading of the Gospel reminds us that the ministry of Jesus touched an enormous number of people. Jesus, in whom the Kingdom of God was fully and abundantly made known, was itinerant. Matthew's Gospel explains that following his baptism in the Jordan and his temptations in the desert, Jesus comes into Galilee and bases himself in Capernaum on the shores of the Sea of Galilee. However, he does not stay there permanently. He rushes from place to place: from North to South and from East to West and back again. He has an ambitious schedule. First, he travels out to other towns and villages of Galilee, crossing the lake from time to time to reach the ten towns: a network of Gentile towns established by the Roman administration. Jesus travels equally towards Caesarea Philippi, and then further and northwards where he enters the region of Tyre and Sidon. Finally, he heads south into the towns and villages of Judea. Here, he enters Jerusalem and is acclaimed by the crowd before being arrested, tried, and put to death. Matthew then tells how the risen Christ also 'travels', appearing first in Jerusalem and then meeting his disciples back where his ministry started: in Galilee to the North. From here he commissions them and sends them out to proclaim the Gospel.

But it is not only Jesus who travels about in order to meet others: others travel to see and hear him from elsewhere. His ministry attracts crowds from places that were not included in his itinerary. Crowds flock to Galilee, drawn to him not only by the authority and quality of his teaching, but also by his power to heal. His reputation has spread far beyond the area that he is able physically to cover himself. Matthew describes how Jesus' reputation extends as far as Syria (Matt. 4:24) and adds that vast numbers of people are attracted to Galilee from every direction. They come from the ten towns and from beyond the Jordan to the East, from the towns and villages of Galilee in the far North and from Judea in the South. The ministry of Jesus reaches an audience far wider and much more diverse than simply the population of Galilee and Jerusalem.

The geographical reach of Jesus' ministry is a concrete expression of his passionate vision of the Kingdom of God. God does not confine his interest to a small group of his favourites. The message of the Kingdom is intended not simply for people who are particularly spiritual or of especially religious disposition, or for those who think they understand the Scriptures better than others. It is not even directed solely to those whose lives might be deemed to be more sinful than others and in special need of help. Instead, God addresses everyone! He freely offers the new life of the Kingdom to poor as well as rich, to young and old, to city- and country-dwellers, regardless of their context, their level of spiritual understanding or their background. The message of the Kingdom of God is magnificently and devastatingly inclusive, pictured as the yeast at work in the *whole* dough of humanity.

Crossing the Boundaries of Gender

The Kingdom of God is open to men and women alike. Undeterred by convention, Jesus receives hospitality and support from both women and men. He accepts invitations not just from men of high social standing, such as Pharisees, but also from women, such as Martha and Mary. His concern for those in need extends not just to men like the crippled man lowered down before him on a stretcher (Mark 2:1–12), but also to women like the one with a haemorrhage (Matt. 9:20–22) and the one unable to stand tall (Luke 13:10–17). Meanwhile, Jesus crosses the boundaries and surprises his disciples by having a profound conversation with a lone Samaritan woman he meets under the midday sun at a well (John 4:6–26).

The first time that Jesus miraculously feeds a crowd with five loaves and two fish, Matthew is careful to specify that five thousand men were present, *not including the women and children* (Matt. 14:21). The second time he feeds a crowd, on this occasion out of a few fish and seven loaves, Matthew recounts that he feeds four thousand and specifies again *not including the women and children* (Matt. 15:38). Matthew is not just emphasising numbers here. Writing at a time in history when only men were really thought to count, Matthew is stressing the fact that it is not just men whose presence is important in the Kingdom of God: women and children are significant also. They have their equal part to play and cannot be made invisible.

Crossing the Boundaries of Expectation

At the time of Jesus, those who were most readily considered to be the most spiritually aware, nearest to God, were those who belonged officially to the religious establishment. However, Matthew's Gospel offers an unexpected—not to say troubling—portrait of the Jewish authorities, such as the scribes, the priests, the Sadducees and the Pharisees. He depicts these characters as those who are, in fact, lacking in faith. The ones who should have been quick to discern the ways of God often show themselves to be nothing short of hypocrites who understand very little of the Kingdom's values,

> "But woe to you, scribes and Pharisees, hypocrites! For you lock people out of the kingdom of heaven. For you

do not go in yourselves, and when others are going in, you stop them" (Matt. 23:13).

On the other hand, those whom the religious authorities think of as unclean: lepers, tax-collectors and prostitutes (Matt. 21:31–32), the lame and the mute (Matt. 15:29–31), are shown in the Gospel narrative to be close to the Kingdom. As Jesus says to his disciples,

> *"Truly I tell you, the tax collectors and the prostitutes are going into the kingdom of God ahead of you"* (Matt. 21:31, NEB).

The Gospels tell us that these 'little people' are almost always those who show evidence of amazing faith. Among them are a large number of women, not least Mary Magdalene, who becomes a witness to the empty tomb, or Martha, the sister of Mary and Lazarus who confesses Jesus to be the Messiah (John 11:27). Another such example is offered by the woman who walks in off the street and washes Jesus' feet with her tears (Luke 7:36–50). Jesus has been invited to a Pharisee's house, and when a woman of ill-repute walks in, the Pharisee is scandalised. Considering himself to be a man of God, he cannot see what could possibly be godly about the likes of such a woman. Jesus, however, sees the presence of the Kingdom at work in her humble attitude and loving action.

In encouraging others to follow him, Jesus does not stay with tradition and remain solely within the company of male disciples. We often forget this. Yet, the Gospel writers tell us that Jesus is followed and supported by women throughout his entire ministry. Luke tells us of the women who followed him even on his way to execution (Luke 23:27–28), while Matthew tells us that women were present at the crucifixion, watching Jesus' death from a distance (Matt. 27:55). They were there!

This is the surprise Jesus has for us. The Kingdom of God is open to one and all, women and men alike, and does not depend on social standing or public reputation. God comes to us just as we are and sees not our past or even our present. Above all, he sees our future as his children, as disciples of Christ and citizens of the Kingdom.

Karla Faye Tucker

Even those written off by a ruthless human justice system and deemed to have no future are offered hope in the whole-heartedly inclusive vision of the Kingdom. Few women better illustrate this than Karla Faye Tucker (1959–1998), a young American woman condemned to death by the court of the state of Texas. In the eyes of the world she had no future. She had been addicted to drugs from the age of 11 and had followed her mother into a life of prostitution. One night in 1983, she went out with her boyfriend with the intention of stealing some motorbike parts from a man they both intensely disliked. Under the influence of drugs, and excited by the thrill of violence, they killed him savagely. As they boasted shamelessly of their exploit to their friends, they were very quickly apprehended and found guilty.

While she was in jail awaiting trial, Karla went to a meeting that had been organised by the prison's chaplaincy team. She was struck by the peace and joy she found there, "They had a peace and a joy—something that was real. I had never seen that in anybody."[3] That night, as she turned the pages of the Bible, she understood the full horror of what she had done. Later she described

---

3   Linda Strom, *Karla Faye Tucker Set Free: Life and Faith on Death Row* (Colorado Springs, CO: Waterbrook Press, 2000), p. 49.

how, as she knelt down begging for forgiveness, she felt the love of God pouring into her.

After that, her life would never be the same again. Something within her had profoundly changed and God's new life so overflowed from her that everyone in the prison noticed the difference. She became involved in the life of the prison's chaplaincy, doing all she could to touch the lives of her fellow-prisoners. She recognised the transformation that had come upon her. "I love life now," she admitted. "Instead of taking lives I just want to share the life in me."[4] The reach of the Kingdom of God had not stopped at the prison gate, or at the door of her cell, and Karla had become its passionate ambassador. After her conversion, Death Row, where she awaited the verdict of human justice with fear in her heart, became the very context in which the yeast of the Kingdom was at work. She renamed it "Life Row". Gradually, the atmosphere in the common room changed. The chaplaincy team visited the prisoners of Life Row at times when they needed to be encouraged. Everyone was welcomed by the warmth of Karla's smile and encouraged and upheld by her prayers. In order to start living for the Kingdom of God, Karla did not wait for her trial to be over or to be released from jail. She did not wait for a time when life would have been better. Death Row became the context in which she offered herself, immediately, as a witness to the Kingdom and as a builder of Kingdom relationships. Through the renewal of her own life, her faith had a dramatic impact on prison life around her.

At the beginning of her Christian life, Karla was greatly encouraged by being forgiven by Peggy, the sister

---

4   Strom, *Karla Faye Tucker Set Free*, 130.

of the man she had murdered. The Sunday after the murder, before the murderer had been identified, Peggy had gone to church as usual. When Peggy walked into the church, the whole church started to pray for the person who had killed her brother. Later, Karla was to believe that it was thanks to the prayers of this church that her life had so radically been changed. Sometime after Karla had been sentenced to death, she received a letter from Peggy. In it, Peggy had written both that she had forgiven Karla, and that she loved her, and asked her to telephone. And so, a fortnight later, Karla rang Peggy. The conversation they had firmly anchored Karla into her new life in Christ. The two women continued to correspond. A very long time afterwards, Peggy spoke honestly about what had happened. She admitted freely that she hated the circumstances in which her brother was killed. "But," she said, "he is in the hands of the Lord. I didn't lose him. I know where he is. Karla became like a little sister to me."[5]

Karla continued to grow in faith, and during the 14 years she spent on Life Row, she lived as an evangelist. In spite of the many voices that testified to her transformation and asked for mercy, George W. Bush, governor of Texas at the time, refused to grant a stay of execution and on 3 February 1998, Karla became the first woman in more than a century to receive the death penalty. On the day of her execution, there were two groups of people waiting outside the prison gates: those who remembered the horror of her crime and felt that the death penalty was a fitting punishment, and those who had seen the transformation that had been at work, and who recognised the passionate and faithful

---

5   Strom, *Karla Faye Tucker Set Free*, 64.

citizen of the Kingdom of God that this young woman had become.

Karla told her friends not to cry for her. "When you've done something like I've done and you've been forgiven for it and you're loved—that has a way of so changing you. I have experienced real love. I know what forgiveness is, even when I've done something so horrible. I know that because God forgave me when I accepted what Jesus did on the cross. When I leave here I'm going to be with Him."[6] Karla often prayed that the Church would look beyond the divisions created by denominations, by race and by prison walls. She knew from her own experience that the yeast of the Kingdom was at work even in the most distant and unlikely part of the dough.

The yeast of the Kingdom can also be at work in us. The extent of the Kingdom does not stop at the door of our heart. Each and every one has a part to play in the life of the Kingdom, no matter our past or our present circumstances. Sometimes we can imagine that our context or our background excludes us from the Kingdom's reach; the memory of past failures and our feelings of guilt can gnaw away at us and make us defensive. If we are accustomed to judging ourselves severely, we can find it difficult to believe that we could possibly be forgiven. Sometimes we can feel so despairing at the course of social and political events that we cannot imagine that opening ourselves to the life of the Kingdom of God could possibly make a difference to anyone or anything.

However, when Jesus announces that the Kingdom of God is at hand, he promises that it will change everything. Those who follow him will experience a new reality: forgiveness and

---

6   Strom, *Karla Faye Tucker Set Free*, 25.

the healing of their hurts; liberation from the vicious circles of their behaviour; a vision of the Kingdom to live by and a life lived according to the values of the Kingdom that are so different from the values by which society lives. To all those who are weary of hearing the bad news of despair and hatred, of injustice and of death in all its manifestations, Jesus says,

> *"Repent, for the kingdom of heaven has come near"*
> *(Matt. 4:17).*

Crossing the Boundaries of Race

Matthew's Gospel has other surprises in store for us. Matthew tells us that throughout the ministry of Jesus, the yeast of the Kingdom is at work not just amongst the Jews in Israel, but also among the Gentiles—people from other nations and ethnicities. Most of the characters in the Gospel are Jews, but there are extraordinary moments when outsiders suddenly come to the fore. They are both men and women. Their presence in the Gospel is a reminder that the Kingdom of God crosses human divides and that God calls people from all nations into the Church of Jesus Christ.

For the people of Israel, Gentiles were people who could not be further from God. Canaanites were associated with the conflicts that had taken place at the time when the Hebrews were entering the promised land. The stories of the great prophets of God, which the people of Israel knew by heart, only served to confirm the idea of Gentiles as worshippers of false gods. Yet at the time of Jesus, the people of Israel were faced with an even more threatening Gentile presence: the occupying forces of the Roman empire. If the Canaanites were thought to worship Baal, the Roman empire—a Gentile empire—worshipped the Roman Emperor himself. Even if the Jewish nation had succeeded in receiving a dispensation from the Roman law that enforced peoples under its jurisdiction to practise the emperor cult, they were nonetheless surrounded by it in the region of the ten towns, on the eastern side of the Sea of Galilee. As far as the people of Israel could see, there was ample reason to believe that the Gentiles had nothing very godly about them.

However, Matthew recounts some extraordinary episodes in his Gospel, in which Gentiles, both men and women, approach Jesus. Even though they come from a very different religious context, they are attracted by the presence of the Kingdom manifested in Jesus and, in coming to him, are touched and changed by him.

Amongst Gentile men who figure in his Gospel, Matthew describes the visit of the wise men who kneel before the baby Jesus and offer him gifts of gold, frankincense and myrrh. These spiritual men recognise in Jesus the presence of a king, the glory of God, and the promise of sacrifice. Matthew tells how after the visit, the wise men "returned home by another road" (Matt. 2:12). By referring to "another road" that the wise men took to return home, Matthew offers a poetic image of the transformation of the wise men. No one can encounter the Christ and not do things differently as a result.

At the start of his ministry in Capernaum, Jesus is approached by a Roman centurion. In the land of Israel, such a man would have been labelled in two ways: first as a Gentile, and worse still, as an enemy of the nation: a servant of the occupying force. Given that Herod, as collaborator with the Romans, employed Gentiles from neighbouring territories as soldiers in the Roman army present in Israel, it is not possible to say whether the centurion comes from Rome itself. But the labels he wears suggest that he would be 'twice removed' from having a relationship with God. However, he has so much faith in Jesus' authority over sickness that he knew Jesus would not even need to enter his house to heal his servant. Jesus expresses the surprising nature of this foreign man's faith when he says,

> "Truly I tell you, in no one in Israel have I found such faith. I tell you, many will come from east and west and will eat with Abraham and Isaac and Jacob in the kingdom of heaven" (Matt. 8:10b–11).

If Matthew offers us a picture of Gentile men at the beginning and in the middle of his Gospel, he also includes the testimony of a Gentile man at the end. The centurion who stands at the cross guarding the prisoner is profoundly touched by the death of Jesus. As a servant of the empire's machinery, this centurion is paid to protect its authority. Yet, even as he does his horrific duty, he movingly utters the confession that other Jewish characters in the story have not made, "Truly, this man was God's son!" (Matt. 27:54).

Gentile women are also noticeably present in the Gospel story. At the very start of his Gospel, Matthew presents us with a genealogy, a list of the generations starting from Abraham, passing through King David and ending up with the birth of Jesus. A traditional family tree would have included only male names, but Matthew breaks out, and includes the names of women. What is more, these are not the names of Hebrew women, but of Gentile women, such as Tamar and Rahab. We shall be looking at these women in more detail in the next chapter.

Later in the Gospel, Jesus is approached by a Canaanite woman. She, too, is a Gentile, and we shall be reading her story in full in Chapter 5. On this occasion, the conversation between Jesus and the woman takes place outside of the land of Israel, in a northern territory that had been disputed for a long time. Jesus recognises in this Gentile also the unexpected presence of faith, "Woman, great is your faith!" (Matt. 15:28).

Meanwhile, at the end of the Gospel, we encounter another Gentile woman: Pilate's wife. Her entry into the story is so brief, we might be in danger of not noticing her presence at all. Yet, as with the centurion, the one-liner role she plays is completely charged with meaning. She advises her husband to have nothing to do with the crucifixion of Jesus. Unlike Jesus' Jewish opponents, this woman deems Jesus to be an "innocent man" (Matt. 27:19). Her dreams, a sign of her spirituality perhaps, have brought her to this point of truthful insight.

The appearance of these significant women in the book of Matthew heralds not just the future presence of Gentiles in the Christian Church, but also Gentile *women*. By including them in his Gospel, Matthew makes it clear that the Christian community of the future will be an inclusive and revolutionary movement that sees men and women as equal witnesses to the Good News of the Gospel.

The extent of the Kingdom is not governed or limited by the presence of geographical borders. It is not confined by boundaries imagined or created by human thinking. There is not a single human being whose life is beyond the scope of the Kingdom of God, no matter their national identity or the colour of their skin. While, all too fearfully, the nations of this world protect their frontiers and their populations with care, employing many hundreds of military personnel or administrative structures to guard the gates of their kingdoms, the Kingdom of God is magnificently open, and its citizens belong to an international community.

Those who belong to the Church are called to point beyond the divisive walls that the world constructs. In recognising that in Christ they are a family, they embrace the openness of the Kingdom and its welcome. Each and every one is a child of God the Father. As such, the North-African and the Syrian, like the American and the Chinese, are brothers in Christ, just as the Palestinian and the Israeli, the Polish and the British, are sisters. It is not a question of simply tolerating those who have a different national identity, or of leaving them be. Neither is it a question of mutual respect, no matter how important such respect might be. As Christians in a Church called to point to the life of the Kingdom, we are called to do more than just respect each other: the call is to love one another as brothers and sisters.

In Christ, we have received a profound identity greater than the one that defines our nationality. For instance, I am British, half English and half Welsh, given that my parents came from different nations within the United Kingdom. Several consequences follow. As they both were English speakers, my mother tongue is English, coloured by the accent typical of someone who grew up in London suburbia. At the same time, I definitely exhibit a Welsh strain of talkativeness and a love of singing. When we are citizens of the Kingdom of God, it is not a question of abandoning our national or cultural identity. On the contrary, these influences root us in human life and shape us distinctly.

But beyond these earthly identities and fidelities, our *Christian* identity influences and defines us more than any other identity. We are called to recognise the authority that is above all others, submit ourselves in obedience to the will of God, and commit to living according to the profound values of the Kingdom. Thus together, as an international community, we witness the action of the yeast that is at work in the dough of the whole world.

Crossing the Divides of Social Background and Political Allegiance

As he goes from place to place, Jesus encounters people who come from a huge range of cultural and social backgrounds. Even in the calling of the twelve, Jesus surrounds himself with a group of people who come from completely different social contexts. First, there are the fishermen: men involved in the commerce of fish and serving principally the population on the shores of the Sea of Galilee. They spend their days on both land and sea, accustomed to reacting quickly to dangerous situations such as storms, and often risk their very lives in order to do their job. They are forced to pay the heavy taxes imposed upon them by the empire, as Peter admits readily when Jesus asks,

> "From whom do kings of the earth take toll or tribute? From their children or from others?" When Peter said, "From others," Jesus said to him, "Then the children are free" (Matt. 17:25b–26).

The Kingdom has not only come near to the fisherman, but also to a tax-collector. The group of disciples gets more interesting. It is not hard to imagine what the fishermen's reaction might have been to the presence of the tax-collector Matthew in the group. When Jesus calls him, Matthew is earning his living as a collaborator with the occupying power. Unlike the fishermen who spend their days risking their lives to earn their crust, Matthew is sitting all day in the tax office, extorting money and lining his pockets with the taxes that the likes of the fishermen have to pay. Worse still, as a tax-collector, Matthew eats with his employers, the Romans, making himself ritually unclean under the law of Moses by his close association with Gentiles.

Jesus also calls Simon, a zealot who in all likelihood belongs to a resistance movement. He is a nationalist, living and networking amongst those who are preparing violent revolution. How did he feel when he discovered the presence of a collaborator in the group of disciples? Matthew never gives us the Curriculum Vitae of all the disciples. But even with the details he does offer, it is possible to understand some of the tensions that exist in the group of disciples and that explode from time to time (Matt. 20:20). However, Christ entrusts the proclamation of the Gospel to this diverse group of disciples who come from a wide range of social and cultural backgrounds.

We find the same mixture of background and social standing in Luke's list of the women who followed Jesus (Luke 8:1–3). First there is Mary of Magdala. Tradition has it that she was a prostitute, although Luke does not specify this. Seven demons had come out of her, so we may assume that prior to her healing she lived as an outcast and was probably not well-off. As she is not described as anyone's wife, she was presumably unmarried. Meanwhile, the town she came from was renowned for its horror of the Roman occupation, and for the violence that had been meted out on its citizens by the Roman army.

In contrast, there is Joanna, the wife of a man who was one of Herod's stewards. Her husband would have been wealthy, no doubt, moving in the higher echelons of society. What is more, Herod was the puppet of the Roman empire, and anyone working for him would have been deemed to be in the pocket of the Romans—a collaborator, even. We can only speculate as to what Joanna thought of Mary of Magdala the first time they were introduced! However, here they are, next to one another in a list, following Jesus shoulder to shoulder.

From the very moment that we accept Christ's invitation to participate in the life of the Kingdom, we never know next to whom we shall end up working and witnessing. Christ always has surprises in store for us, often placing us alongside people who are vastly different from us. But that is exactly the point: in a world torn by divisions of all kinds, our unity in Christ plays an essential part in our witness to the Kingdom, whatever our social, cultural or national differences may be.

Perpetua and Felicitas

Already in the first centuries, Christians faithful to the Gospel scandalised the societies from which they came by witnessing to the extraordinary values of the Kingdom: worshipping and eating together, the rich alongside the poor, the free alongside slaves. I am always very moved every time I read the story of Perpetua, a young Christian woman from North Africa who lived at the beginning of the third century. As a member of a patrician family, she belonged to the upper echelons of Carthaginian society. The city was a Roman colony. Her family had a high reputation in the eyes of the Roman authorities and took great care to protect it.

In the first centuries, it was rare for people in high society to become Christians. However, Perpetua was converted, and with her, her slave Felicitas. In the company of other Christians, they were both arrested, imprisoned and condemned to death. From the very start of the story, these two women, with diametrically opposed social positions, witnessed to their faith in Christ side by side.

To our knowledge, Perpetua is the first Christian woman to have kept a spiritual journal. Coming from a high social position, she had learnt to read and write. This was very rare for a woman at the time. The young slave with whom she was imprisoned was eight months pregnant. Roman law forbade the execution of a pregnant woman, and delayed an execution until after the birth had taken place. Felicitas was terrified that if she did not give birth before the execution day, she would not be able to meet her death alongside the other Christian prisoners. If her martyrdom were delayed, she would then be put to death alongside a number of common criminals and her Christian witness would be compromised. Alongside the other Christians, mistress and slave spent the night in humble prayer, asking that the baby be born in the coming hours. Thanks be to God! Their prayer was answered.

During the first centuries after the resurrection, depending on the region and the governor in question, Christians were sporadically, but often very severely, persecuted. The teaching of Jesus had warned his disciples about it. Jesus had prepared his followers for the day when they would find themselves standing in a tribunal, on trial for their faith. The Roman empire decreed that all its subjects should recognise the Emperor as Lord by making sacrifices. In the first century, the Romans made an exception for the Jews and also for Christians in the earliest days of the Church, given that the first Christians were also Jews.

However, as soon as Gentiles started to be welcomed in their numbers into the Church, the Christian community was expelled from the Jewish community and no longer benefitted from the dispensation from Emperor worship accorded to the Jewish nation. Christians categorically refused to recognise the Roman Emperor as Lord, and their refusal was seen by the empire as the ultimate treason. Many were put to death. The Christians understood their execution as the most powerful moment of their Christian witness. The Greek for 'witness' is in fact the word 'martyr'. Today, we use the word 'martyr' to describe someone who gives their life for their faith, but in the first days, a 'martyr' was simply a witness. It was well known that a Christian's faithfulness to the values of the Kingdom might lead inevitably to death.

Perpetua had a baby whom she was still breastfeeding at the time of her arrest. She was faced with the devastating choice between renouncing her faith, keeping her baby and the love of her father, and remaining faithful to Christ, losing her child and the approval of her father. It was a profound spiritual battle between the different identities of her life. As a daughter, she owed her allegiance and obedience to her father, and had no wish to threaten the good standing of the family in patrician society and drag its reputation into the mire. As a mother, she wanted to be faithful to her newborn baby. Having spent the night in prayer and having received a vision that she recounts powerfully in her journal, she had the strength to stand before the governor and affirm her principal identity in a calm, assured voice. When the governor asked her if she was a Christian, she simply replied, "Yes".[7]

Together with the other Christians, our two courageous women were led into the arena where, according to the custom, the spectators were positioned according to their social position: the richest in the best seats. Before being thrown to the wild beasts, the Christians stopped to witness to their faith by a specific act. In front of all the spectators, these men and women from different social backgrounds, from the greatest to the very least, Perpetua and Felicitas among them, challenged the dignity of the Roman empire by exchanging a kiss of peace. Perpetua and Felicitas had understood that we do not witness to the Kingdom by

---

7 Bruno Chenu, Claude Prud'homme, France Quéré, Jean-Claude Thomas, *The Book of Christian Martyrs* (New York, NY: Crossroad, 1990), p. 65.

division, but by our unity, for in Christ,

> *There is no longer Jew or Greek, there is no longer slave or free, there is no longer male and female; for all of you are one in Christ Jesus (Gal. 3:28).*

The testimony of Perpetua reminds us that we each have multiple identities. The first, above all others, is our identity in Christ, which orientates us towards the Kingdom. But, of course, we have others, dependent on the different social contexts in which we live and move. There are the identities that define our private life, such as son or daughter, wife or husband, mother or father, brother or sister, friend or partner. The context for these identities is the home, the street or the town in which we live. Then there are those identities that define our church life: whether we are Methodist or Moravian, Mennonite or Catholic, Anglican or Baptist. The context for these identities is the local church or the parish, the diocese or the particular alliance of churches. Similarly, there are identities that define our working life: nurse, managing director, cleaner, cashier, scientist, librarian etc. These in their turn are lived out in different contexts, such as the hospital, the office, the supermarket, the laboratory, or the library. And then there are the identities that come from our leisure activities, which are played out in the community space or the leisure centre, the cinema or the café.

Each of these contexts is the place in which we witness to our allegiance to the Kingdom of God. In the course of my life, I have had the opportunity to work with churches from a wide variety of Christian traditions. It has been an immense privilege to meet Christians from every type of spirituality and worship-style. Very often I ask others where they see the

Kingdom of God at work in their lives, and am always struck that their replies usually focus either on their family life or on their church life. I receive the answer that their son has become a Christian, or that their marriage has grown deeper. With a big smile, people tell me that there are more people coming to church than three years ago, that the Bible Studies are deeper than they used to be or that there is a higher attendance at house groups. Answers rarely go further than this.

However, if we allow ourselves to be challenged by our parable, which reminds us that the yeast is at work in the *whole* dough, we need to recognise that there is no place in which we might not expect to the see the Kingdom of God at work. The ministry of Jesus points to this clearly. As he goes from place to place, Jesus does not rush immediately to the centres of worship—the synagogues—even if he goes there from time to time to teach or to heal. Rather, Matthew depicts Jesus out in the public sphere, surrounded by the crowds, on the hillside (Matt. 15:29) or in the desert (Matt. 14:13), on the shores of the lake (Matt. 13:1) or on the road (Matt. 15:21). There are moments when he enters a house: he visits the home of disciples (Matt. 8:14; 9:10), of people who ask him to heal members of their family (Matt. 9:18; 9:27) or of the people who offer him protection or hospitality (Matt. 26:6). However, Jesus never stays constantly with his disciples behind the closed doors of a classroom, but invites them to follow his itinerary. They share the moments when their master addresses his teaching to the whole crowd, and, in turn, are sent out into other places to announce the Good News of the Kingdom.

Jesus is faithful to his name Emmanuel, God with us. A carpenter by trade, he is fully rooted in the life of the people. He selects disciples from different walks of life, and also encounters people from an even greater range of social backgrounds during the course of his ministry—from political and religious leaders to ordinary people from town and country, and from the rich who enjoy good food and splendid clothes (Matt. 6:25–26) to the poor they neglect (Matt. 19:21–22). He meets the sick and the healthy, those who are excluded from society as well as those who exclude them. He engages as much with those who agree with him and who want to learn more, as with those who approach him asking simply for a cure, or who are not interested in believing, and even with those who are violently opposed to him. The ninth chapter of Matthew, for example, offers us a picture of a ministry, which from one hour to the next takes Jesus from the top to the bottom of the social ladder. First, he is approached by a Jewish officer who asks him to come and heal his daughter. But on his way to his house, he heals a woman whose condition places her at the very margins of society. He eventually reaches the officer's house, goes inside to heal the girl, and, on leaving, encounters two blind men on the road.

> We are called to look for the signs of the Kingdom in every context: in our hospitals, our schools, in our prisons, not to mention the worlds of politics and finance, in the arts and the sciences.

Now, of course it is important to recognise the presence of God's Kingdom at work in our family life and in the life of our churches. But the extent of the Kingdom of God is far bigger than that. As the ministry of Jesus clearly shows us, the Kingdom is not the monopoly of one small group. There are countless opportunities in our lives as Christians where we are invited actively to participate in the life of the Kingdom of God, which is at work in all the places in which we find ourselves. We are called to look for the signs of the Kingdom in every context: in our hospitals, our schools, in our prisons, not to mention the worlds of politics and finance, in the arts and the sciences. God will not be imprisoned by the walls built by our fears, our rigid traditions or engrained comfort-zones. Like the yeast, the Kingdom is already at work in hearts and lives in every place, and in his great generosity, God invites us to collaborate with him: *Then he said to his disciples, "The harvest is plentiful, but the laborers are few; therefore ask the Lord of the harvest to send out laborers into his harvest"* (Matt. 9:37–38).

Matthew tells how Jesus adapts his teaching with care and wisdom to his listeners, depending on their social context. During his ministry in the agricultural region of Galilee, his teaching uses images taken from an agricultural context. In his parables, he talks about the sower and the wheat, seeds and fields, fish, pearls and sheep. Once he arrives in Jerusalem, the capital, his images reflect the life of the city, and the parables revolve around debts and the world of finance, and talk about palaces and royal banquets, investments and the servants who have to manage their master's affairs when he is away. The variety of images that he uses enables him to speak to the greatest number of people, while his message remains the same: The Kingdom of God is at hand. As the parable of the wedding-feast describes, the invitation to participate in the life of the Kingdom is offered to each and every one, whatever their social context. The invitation is open to good and bad alike.

Now, there are those whom God calls into mission and whom he sends to other countries to serve him: there is no question. But we do not have to wait to receive a call to serve on the other side of the world to understand that we are already called into mission. We are already ambassadors of the Kingdom of God in the very places in which we live our lives: in the corridors of the town hall, at the bank, in the café, in our homes. In his faithfulness, God is always seeking to offer in and through us the profound and dynamic picture of the yeast of the Kingdom at work in all the dough, made known in the landscapes of our lives.

The women whom we meet in the course of Matthew's Gospel offer us a very moving portrait of the Kingdom of heaven at work, transforming human lives. Coming from different places—from Galilee, Tyre and Sidon, Rome and Judaea—and from different family situations, they also represent different cultural milieus—rich and poor, influential and marginalised. But in one sense or another, each one of them is open to the presence of the Kingdom of God made known in Jesus. Each one of them is touched and challenged to live out the values of that Kingdom in the contexts in which God has placed them.

In the chapters of this book, we will come to know these exceptional women in a new way as we seek the elements of the Kingdom of God, at work like the yeast, in their relationship with Jesus and with others. But before we move into this fascinating and inspiring study, we will take a moment to glance at the women whose names appear in the genealogy of Jesus and whose lives, centuries before, anticipated the values of God's Kingdom.

2 SEEKING SIGNS: THE MYSTERIOUS KINGDOM

There is no place in my soul, no corner of my character, where God is not.
Evelyn Underhill[8]

Lots of His work is done in the dark, in secret, underground.
Muriel Lester[9]

When he speaks of the action of the woman as she mixes the dough, Jesus uses surprising language. Most translations of the Gospel explain that a woman "took and mixed" the yeast with flour. Of course, when we read this, we have no trouble understanding what kind of action is being described.

However, Jesus' choice of words here is very striking, as in fact he speaks of the yeast that a woman took and "hid" in three measures of flour. Such language might seem rather strange. We rarely talk of "hiding" our sugar in a cup of tea or "hiding" eggs in a cake mixture. However, the use of this word offers a perfect description of the disappearance of the yeast, which, once dissolved in water and mixed in with the flour,

---

8   (1875–1941), British theologian, writer and spiritual guide.
9   (1883–1968), British community builder, advocate of justice and peace, travelling secretary for the Fellowship of Reconciliation.

becomes invisible to the baker. The yeast is nonetheless very much at work, hidden in the depths of the dough. The effect of its action will soon be visible.

Jesus' carefully chosen words lead us into the mystery of the Kingdom, which is at work in secret, in the depths of the soul and the darkest corners of the world, beavering away for a long time before the effects of its presence are made known. The presence of the Kingdom may be discerned by those who look with faith into the very heart of things. But otherwise, to those who look only on the surface, the yeast of the Kingdom remains hidden, neither noticed nor understood. We belong to a society that increasingly judges value by the most superficial of appearances, and Jesus has a great deal to teach us in this parable.

> *"The kingdom of heaven is like treasure hidden in a field, which someone found and hid; then in his joy he goes and sells all that he has and buys that field" (Matt. 13:44).*

And even if our gospel is veiled, it is veiled to those who are perishing. In their case the god of this world has blinded the minds of the unbelievers, to keep them from seeing the light of the gospel of the glory of Christ, who is the image of God (2 Cor. 4:3–4).

Hidden in History: The Women of the Genealogy (Matt. 1:1–17)

Right at the outset of his Gospel, Matthew mentions a number of women whose presence at first sight is astonishing. The first chapter of Matthew opens on a genealogy: a long list of names down the generations, leading to the birth of the Messiah. This genealogy is very Jewish in nature: it begins with Abraham, the father of the nation, and travels through the generations up to King David, before recounting the subsequent generations leading to the birth of Christ.

Amidst the long list of illustrious patriarchs, a number of women's names are to be found. Already it is strange and entirely unexpected to find such names included in a genealogy, which would figure only men's names in normal circumstances. What is more, it is equally strange that Matthew should have chosen the names of these particular women, rather than opting to include those who might seem more important or significant, such as Sarah or Rebecca. However, the likes of Sarah and Rebecca do not figure at all, and the reader of the Gospel might be forgiven for thinking that Matthew's choice is rather bizarre.

First of all, Matthew mentions Tamar, whose story is told in the book of Genesis. Then he lists Rahab, who appears in the book of Joshua; Ruth, who has a book named after her; and Bathsheba from I Kings. Finally, he names Mary, the mother of Jesus. So why does Matthew incorporate these particular women in his genealogy? What do these women have in common that has led to their inclusion on the list? Is there a theme that links their lives together?

All Outsiders

At first sight, as we mentioned in Chapter I, it is clear that each of these women is from a Gentile background. Tamar, the daughter-in-law of Judah, is a Canaanite, as is Rahab, who is an inhabitant of Jericho. Ruth originates from the kingdom of Moab, to the East. The Scriptures do not tell us where Bathsheba comes from, but the fact that she is married to Uriah the Hittite—a Gentile—implies that she was considered to be a Gentile by her marriage to Uriah. Mary follows the pattern also in part: coming from Galilee in the North, she is considered, in Matthew's Jewish perspective, to belong to a Gentile region.

So, looking first at the geographical origins of these women, we might want already to conclude, along with a large number of Biblical scholars, that listing these women in the genealogy points to the inclusive nature of the Kingdom of God. These foreign women also prefigure the welcome of Gentiles into the Church and demonstrate from the very beginning of the Gospel that, as we saw in the previous chapter, nobody is beyond the reach of the Kingdom.

But what else might these women have in common? Might we find something beyond their Gentile identity that might link these women, either one to another, or to the proclamation of the Gospel? In order to answer this question, let us look a little more closely at each of the passages in which the stories of the women are told.

Tamar: Incestuous Widow (Gen. 38:1–30)

If we were to glance at the story of Tamar in a fairly superficial way, we might come up with a reading something like this,

The Canaanite woman Tamar is Judah's daughter-in law. Her husband dies without leaving a son. The levirate law of the time demands that she be given to one of her deceased husband's brothers, whose duty it is to raise up sons for his dead brother as inheritors of his property. However, the second brother to whom Tamar is given dies prematurely without having provided a son for his brother. Judah refuses to give Tamar to his third son and sends her back to her father's house a widow, where she plots revenge. Sometime afterwards, Tamar disguises herself as a prostitute, and lures her own father-in-law into her bed without disclosing her true identity. By this calculating trick and incestuous act, Tamar becomes pregnant and gives birth to twin sons.

This is a story full of drama. At first sight it is easy to be scandalised by the behaviour of this widow who, instead of obeying Judah and staying quietly and respectfully at her father's house, spends her time wickedly concocting a plot to trap her father-in-law into bed. She tricks her father-in-law by disguising herself as a prostitute and draws him into a mire of incest without his knowledge. In so doing, she degrades herself and risks the good reputation of her family. If we were to accept this interpretation, we might well judge Tamar to be devoid of any moral conscience or spiritual sensitivity.

However, when we take the trouble to look more closely at this story in its ancient context, other exciting perspectives emerge. First of all, a close reading of Judah's story reveals that this man is far from being faithful and just before God. Even when his father Jacob had insisted on the importance of not marrying a Canaanite woman, he ignored his advice and married Bathshua without asking for his father's consent or blessing (Gen. 38:2). Already a considerable lack of faithfulness on his part! If he is present at the birth of his first son in order to name him, he leaves the task to his wife for the birth of the next two sons. Moreover, at the time of the third birth, he appears to have left the family altogether for Keziv, an area whose name means 'place of lies'. So already the portrait of Judah is not exactly flattering.

Nor does it improve. After burying his first two sons, he should according to levirate law keep Tamar in his household and give her his third son. But Judah is scared of losing him, and making an excuse on account of his son's youth, orders his daughter-in-law to return to her father's house. He behaves as if she no longer exists for him, and condemns her to a widowhood which was associated with poverty and low social standing at the time. Sometime later, we meet him again, this time easily drawn into bed with a woman he takes to be a prostitute. When he discovers that Tamar is pregnant, he is unaware that she is carrying his child and is ready to have her burnt to save the reputation of the family. As a man belonging to the people of God, we might surely have expected something better of him.

His sons are barely an improvement. Although the passage does not provide many details of the life of Er, it offers enough, stating plainly, "But Er, Judah's firstborn, was wicked in the sight of the Lord, and the Lord put him to death" (Gen. 38:7).

He has not been faithful in the ways of God and the author allows us to imagine the kind of life he led. Meanwhile, the second son, Onan, regularly has sexual relations with Tamar but spills his seed on the ground "so that he would not give offspring to his brother" (Gen. 38:9). He is dishonest: a trickster. He gives the impression of doing his duty according to levirate Law but is really not obedient to it at all. After the death of Onan, the third brother does not fulfil his responsibility to Tamar by marrying her either.

So, these four Hebrew men are all far from fulfilling their duties with regard to the Law. On the contrary, they each behave in a way that disregards the Law, and treats Tamar without the justice she deserves. Meanwhile, Tamar, the Canaanite, goaded into action by her extreme circumstances, does end up fulfilling her duty with regard to God's law. She succeeds in saving the line of which Judah was careless, and God permits her to become pregnant by her father-in-law, thus assuring the line. She goes from a place of death as a widow to the place of life, as one who is able to bear children to her deceased husband.

The great surprise of the story comes at the dramatic moment in which Judah discovers the truth of what has happened. With honesty, he recognises that he has fallen short in his duty and affirms the reality of the situation, "She is more in the right than I, since I did not give her to my son Shelah" (Gen. 38:26).

His words highlight the contrast between the behaviour of Tamar—the Canaanite who remains essentially faithful to the levirate law and continues her husband's lineage—and that of Judah. It is Tamar and not Judah who is more 'just', or more 'in the right'. The narrator of this passage of Genesis does not judge Tamar severely. She gives birth to two sons. In the context of the story of Genesis, these births represent a real sign of God's blessing upon her.

The Hebrew word for 'just' (also translatable by the word 'righteous'), which is used in this passage to describe Tamar's actions, appears very often in the Hebrew scriptures in relation to the justice, or righteousness, of God,

> *The Lord's judgements are true and **righteous** every one (Ps. 19:9b, REB).*

> *Against you only have I sinned*
> *and have done what displeases;*
> *you are **right** when you accuse me*
> *and justified in passing sentence (Ps. 51:4, REB).*

If we move from the book of Genesis back into the Gospel of Matthew, we find that **justice**, or **righteousness**,[10] is a key theme for Matthew throughout the Gospel in speaking of the Kingdom of God,

> *"Blessed are those who hunger and thirst for **righteousness**, for they shall be satisfied" (Matt. 5:6, RSV).*

> *"Blessed are those who are persecuted for **righteousness**' sake, for theirs is the kingdom of heaven" (Matt. 5:10, RSV).*

---

10   These English words are both used to translate the Greek word 'δικαιόσυνη'.

> *"Yet wisdom is **justified** by her deeds" (Matt. 11:19c, RSV).*

The same word is intimately linked with the Kingdom in Jesus' teaching,

> *"For I tell you, unless your **righteousness** exceeds that of the scribes and Pharisees, you will never enter the kingdom of heaven" (Matt. 5:20, RSV).*

> *"Set your mind on God's kingdom and his **justice** before everything else, and all the rest will come to you as well" (Matt. 6:33, REB).*

These links might suggest to us that Tamar is included in the genealogy not solely because she is an outsider. Her presence reminds us that *even as an outsider* she lives according to values that point to the Kingdom of God.[11] Certainly her life is far from simple and confronted with the customs and traditions of her time, she is driven by her powerlessness to commit acts that are not usually associated with a typical woman of God! However, justice, or righteousness, is still present in her life, hidden behind the injustice of Judah. The text readily acknowledges it in Judah's own words.

The reading of such a passage warns us against judging a woman or man of the Bible according to the values, ideas or expectations of our own times. We are no longer governed by laws that decree that the sole purpose of a woman's life is to bear children to her husband and assure the family line. We can be in danger of being blind to God by looking through our own cultural spectacles at the surface of a Biblical narrative. The portrait of Tamar has invited us to seek the hidden values

---

11 E. Anne Clements, *Mothers on the Margin?: The Significance of the Women in Matthew's Genealogy* (Eugene, OR: Pickwick Publications), pp. 63–67.

of the Kingdom in the Biblical narrative. It has warned us to become more conscious of the prejudices and expectations that can prevent us from seeing the yeast of the Kingdom at work in the most unexpected of places.

Rahab: Prostitute of an Enemy People (Josh. 2; 6)

If we were to throw a cursory glance over this passage, we might arrive at an interpretation of it like this,

> The Canaanite prostitute Rahab attracts two gentlemen clients to her home. These men are in fact spies, sent by Joshua to reconnoitre the land in advance of a military assault by the people of Israel. When she learns their true identity, Rahab saves them from danger with the intention of using her help as a bargaining tool later on. Wanting to escape inevitable death when her city is defeated, she bargains with the men promising to protect them on condition that they offer her the same protection when Joshua's army is victorious.

However, if we were to look for the values of the Kingdom in this passage, we would find as much for Rahab as we did for Tamar, that the story is considerably less straightforward than it first appears. In the first place, the book of Joshua recounts how Joshua sends spies out from Sittim. According to the book of Numbers, it was at Sittim that the Israelites first had sexual relations (the text says that they prostituted themselves) with Moabite women who encouraged them to offer sacrifices to their gods. The mention of such a notorious place in Rahab's story might lead us to believe that Rahab may well be about to do the same thing, and lead the spies into worshipping false gods.

Rahab, however, does nothing of the kind. In fact, she does quite the opposite. The spies from Israel show very little obedience to the simple commandments of Joshua. As soon as they arrive in the city, they hurry to a brothel in order to combine pleasure with their work. After that, they show themselves to be selfish in acting first and foremost to save their own skins. Meanwhile, Rahab risks all in order to save the life of these spies, putting her own life in danger by lying to the king, hiding the men in her house and helping them escape by letting them down the other side of the wall with the rope. What extraordinary courage! Later, in stark contrast to the spies who say nothing, it is Rahab who declares her faith, affirming the great acts of God who freed his people from slavery. It is Rahab who recognises the power and glory of God when she says, "The Lord your God is indeed God in heaven above and on earth below" (Josh. 2:11b).

She accounts for her action of saving the lives of the spies in terms of faithfulness and loving kindness, and in return she reasonably expects them to show the same loving kindness towards her as she has demonstrated towards them. She says, "Now swear to me by the Lord that you will show kindness to my family, because I have shown kindness to you" (Josh. 2:12, NIV).

The words that she uses here are found countless times in the Hebrew scriptures. The Psalms, for example, speak repeatedly of the 'loving kindness' or the 'mercy' of God. We know these verses by heart,

> *Goodness and **love unfailing**, these will follow me all the days of my life (Ps. 23:6, NEB).*

> *Have mercy on me, O God, according to your **steadfast love** (Ps. 51:1a).*

> *For the Lord is good; and **his steadfast love** endures forever, and his faithfulness to all generations (Ps. 100:5).*

It is this same word that describes the relationship between God and his people,

> *The Lord descended in the cloud and stood with him there, and proclaimed the name, "The Lord." The Lord passed before him, and proclaimed,*
> *"The Lord, the Lord,*
> *a God merciful and gracious,*
> *slow to anger,*
> *and abounding in steadfast love and faithfulness,*
> *keeping steadfast love for the thousandth generation,*
> *forgiving iniquity and transgression and sin ..." (Ex. 34:5–7a).*

The same loving kindness must also characterise the relationships between people. When it should have been the spies who offered an example of true godly conduct to Rahab, we find that she is the one who shows evidence of this essential quality of faithfulness. This story presents us with the extraordinary example of a Canaanite prostitute who demonstrates both faith and faithfulness.

This same keyword, in its Greek translation, is present in the Gospel of Matthew, even if the translations do not always highlight it,

> *"Blessed are the **merciful**, for they will receive **mercy**" (Matt. 5:7).*

> *"Go and learn what this means, 'I desire **mercy**, not sacrifice'" (Matt. 9:13).*

*"Should you not to have had **mercy** on your fellow slave, as I had mercy on you?" (Matt. 18:33).*

So, Rahab is not only the outsider who signifies the welcome of Gentiles into the Church and who reminds us again that the Kingdom of God is not limited by human boundaries. Outsider that she is, she also overturns our expectations by exemplifying values of the Kingdom that are fully and perfectly present in Jesus. The label of 'prostitute' might lead us to expect nothing but sinfulness. But hidden beneath it, the values of the Kingdom of God are already abundantly at work in the life of this Gentile woman.[12]

One of my colleagues works as a chaplain in one of the largest men's prisons in the country. People are always asking him why he has chosen to surround himself with 'criminals'. He responds to them by assuring them that he is surrounded rather by human beings. "Certainly," he said to me, "each one has committed a crime and it is important that crime should be dealt with by our judicial system. It's equally essential that the prisoner takes responsibility for his action. But behind all the labels, each one is worth far more than the sum of his worst acts." In his ministry, my colleague believes himself to be an agent of the Kingdom, seeking the signs of the Kingdom and building it up even in the darkest corners of the prison.

The words of my colleague are reminiscent of Karla's story, which we looked at in Chapter I. The day of her conversion, she took a Bible from the chaplaincy department and took it back to her cell. As she could not imagine that Bibles were given out freely, she imagined that she was stealing it. She had such a strong desire to experience the life and love of God for herself that she did not hesitate to launch into another criminal act. But behind her thieving intentions, the yeast of the Kingdom was already at work: hidden perhaps, but at work none the less.

---

12   Clements, *Mothers on the Margin?*, 91–95.

When we reflect on the quality of our own lives, we are more than uncomfortably aware that the values of the Kingdom are all too often pushed out by our weakness and sinfulness. We stand constantly in need of God's mercy and forgiveness to be pardoned and restored. Yet, thanks be to God, the yeast is at work in the darkest corners of our hearts and each one of us is worth more than the sum of the actions that we most regret. The story of Rahab invites us to seek the yeast of the Kingdom at work in the lives of others, hidden beneath the labels that we know all too well: immigrant, good-for-nothing, druggy, drunk and so many others. Those who truly seek the yeast of the Kingdom active in the lives of others will not be disappointed.

Ruth: Dependent Immigrant (Ruth 1–4)

Let us move on to look at Ruth, the third woman cited in the genealogy. If we were to read the story of Ruth without much care, we might arrive at a reading like this,

> Without hope of bearing children through levirate law, Ruth is a widow who has been reduced to poverty by famine. Instead of staying in her native country as her widowed sister-in-law does, Ruth decides to seek a better life and travels to the land of Israel as a refugee. She comes with her mother-in-law, herself the widow of a man from Bethlehem. Learning that a wealthy landowner in the area is a family member, she engineers to glean on his land. Then one night, following her mother-in-law's prompting, she bathes and perfumes herself before entering Boaz's tent. He is asleep having eaten and drunk well. She lies down at his feet. When he wakes, she introduces herself to him not

as a widow but as 'his servant'. As a result of this scandalous ruse, she succeeds in becoming Boaz's wife and enjoys an undeservedly prosperous and well-to-do life-style.

By now we will not be surprised to discover that a closer reading of the passage leads us to see this woman in a different light. The book of Ruth is full of the theme of faithfulness. The story essentially focuses on the relationship between two women. Firstly, there is Naomi, the widow of the Israelite Elimelec, who had fled poverty in Israel and made a home in Moab. Secondly, there is Ruth, her daughter-in-law. According to levirate law, Elimelec's family should have married Ruth to her brother-in-law, but he also has died and left his own widow equally childless. When famine strikes, Naomi takes the decision to return to Israel. Her two daughters-in-law start out with her. On their way, Naomi frees the two young women from their obligation towards their husband's family. She knows that she cannot provide them with the sons who could marry them and assure the family line. She freely acknowledges the faithfulness that these two Moabite women have shown to her family,

> *But Naomi said to her two daughters-in-law, "Go back each of you to your mother's house. May the Lord deal kindly with you, as you have dealt with the dead and with me." (Ruth 1:8).*

The first daughter-in-law takes the decision to stay in Moab. Ruth, on the other hand, fervently expresses her desire to remain with her mother-in-law. It is a stupendous decision. She categorically refuses to stay in Moab where perhaps, despite the famine, she might find another husband. Instead, at the risk of destitution, she remains faithful to her husband's family. She chooses to renounce her own family ties, her national identity and her gods in order to stay with her mother-in-law who, in return, has nothing to offer except her poverty and her bitterness towards God. A young widow, a vulnerable immigrant, Ruth gives voice to an astounding faithfulness towards Naomi and her God,

> *Where you go, I will go;*
> *where you lodge, I will lodge;*
> *your people shall be my people,*
> *and your God my God.*
> *Where you die, I will die—there will I be buried*
> *(Ruth 1:16b–17a).*

Once in Bethlehem, Ruth perseveres in faithfulness towards Naomi by gleaning a living for them both. One day, on her return from the fields, Ruth recounts to Naomi that she has been able to work on Boaz's land. He has been generous to her. Boaz is a "kinsman", a relative of Naomi's deceased husband. Hearing this news, Naomi is overjoyed. She immediately understands that Boaz has shown commitment to family ties. She can already see a levirate marriage, of Ruth to Boaz, on the horizon. Such a marriage would lead to the birth of sons, who would ensure the line of Naomi's deceased son (Ruth's deceased husband) and safeguard his inheritance. It would also redeem both Ruth and herself from isolation and poverty. Naomi reacts in the same way as before, recognising the faithfulness of God, "Blessed be he by the Lord, whose kindness has not forsaken the living or the dead!" (Ruth 2:20). For Naomi, God's faithfulness has been expressed not only through Ruth's faithfulness to her but now also through Ruth's meeting with Boaz.

Naomi and Ruth take matters into their own hands. Sometime later, Ruth has the courage to go down to the threshing-floor at night and lie at Boaz's feet. When he wakes up, she presents herself to him as his "servant". In short, she challenges him to play the kinsman role and marry her. Boaz agrees.

It is not only Naomi who recognises Ruth's faithfulness. Boaz also does. He sees that Ruth, a foreigner, is committed to her mother-in-law, to the family of her deceased husband, and through this, to the Lord. As well as this, he knows that Ruth's fidelity is a reminder of the Lord's faithfulness and a sign of his blessing,

> *He said, "May you be blessed by the Lord, my daughter; this last instance of your loyalty is better than the first; you have not gone after young men, whether poor or rich" (Ruth 3:10).*

Boaz, who is also an upright and faithful man, marries Ruth precisely because he sees in her this very virtue of faithfulness. Strikingly unlike the brothers-in-law of Tamar whose story we read earlier in this chapter, Boaz wholeheartedly fulfils his duty to the levirate law and Ruth becomes the Gentile grandmother of King David. She gives Naomi a grandchild for her old age and assures the family line of her husband Elimelec, whose name means 'God is King'. Thanks to her faithfulness, isolation is transformed into community and hopelessness into joy.

In taking the decision to accompany Naomi, Ruth foreshadows the very qualities of the faithful disciple of the Kingdom of God who is invited to leave all to follow Jesus,

> *Then Jesus told his disciples, "If any want to become my followers, let them deny themselves and take up their cross and follow me" (Matt. 16:24).*

> *And he said to them, "Follow me, and I will make you fish for people." Immediately they left their nets and followed him (Matt. 4:19–20).*

> *But Jesus said to him, "Follow me, and let the dead bury their own dead" (Matt. 8:22).*

A disciple is also called to go the second mile,

> *"And if anyone forces you to go one mile, go also the second mile" (Matt. 5:41).*

Like so many other Biblical figures, Ruth embodies the extraordinary faith of the poorest people of the earth whose great dignity often gets hidden beneath the unjust prejudices of the rich world. She finds a place in this genealogy not just because she is an outsider, but also because she puts into practice (more than her Israelite mother-in-law) the faithfulness that is at the heart of God's relationship with his people.[13] This kind of loving faithfulness will be made known in Jesus.

Interestingly, the book of Ruth rarely speaks directly about the action or the word of God. Certainly, there are strong references to the Lord, but he never intervenes in the same way as he does, for example, in the stories of Moses, Elijah or Jonah. Rather, the book of Ruth is in a sense far subtler, leaving the reader the task of seeking the yeast of the Kingdom at work in the lives of the Biblical figures. There is no doubt that the presence of the Kingdom is well and truly manifest in the life of this refugee immigrant: an extraordinary woman of God.

Bathsheba: Pregnant Outside Marriage (2 Samuel 11–12:25)

Down the centuries, Bathsheba has undoubtedly developed

---
13   Clements, *Mothers on the Margin?*, 116–120.

a reputation for being both a calculating seductress and outrageous sinner. She has been portrayed as such by many a painter and sculptor. If we were to allow ourselves to be influenced by these portrayals, we might come up with a reading of the story like this,

> Taking advantage of her husband's absence on a military campaign, Bathsheba, an ambitious woman, bathes alluringly on the roof of her house and seduces David, the King of Israel. She cunningly attracts his gaze, excites his desire, and incites him to commit adultery with her. She becomes pregnant and when her husband dies, she brings her wicked plot to fruition and succeeds in becoming the king's wife. The newborn lives only for a few days, but Bathsheba becomes pregnant again and gives birth to a second child.

However, on reading the text more carefully, we again discover another side to the story. First of all, with the exception of one instance, this woman is named throughout the story not by her own name, but by the Hebrew expression 'she of Uriah.' With its patriarchal view of the world, the story invites us to see Bathsheba as principally the dependent of Uriah. She is his chattel. That she should be named in this way highlights the fact that the two principal characters in this story are not David and Bathsheba, but actually David and Uriah. David is the king of Israel and Uriah is a Hittite. Bathsheba is in third position, as the wife of this outsider.

Often, we think of David as the courageous servant of God, who as a shepherd boy confronts and slays Goliath, or as the great poet whose psalms speak powerfully of our relationship with God. Here, however, in a story that takes place during a time of war, the picture of David is far less flattering. David has sent Joab and all his servants and all Israel on campaign. All of them are showing faithfulness to the nation and risking their very lives for it. However, instead of accompanying them all into battle and putting his life at risk for his people, David has evidently stayed behind in the safety of Jerusalem. He is not even busily engaged in the affairs of state, but spending his days in idleness, getting up only at evening. Not a very good start! The fact of the matter is that David should not even have been in the city at this time. Already, this is a king who lacks the fidelity he should rightfully show towards the nation.

According to the Law of Moses, adultery is an act of theft committed by one man against another, the first man depriving the second of his rightful property. The passage describes an offence committed by David *against Uriah*—the husband of Bathsheba—and describes the sexual act from David's point of view. As the parable of Nathan makes clear later on in the story, the woman—whom Nathan compares to a lamb in the parable—is not considered as an actor in the event. Since the king looks down on Bathsheba's bathing from above, it is not even clear whether Bathsheba knows that she is being observed. The writer does not specify whether Bathsheba knows that David is in Jerusalem, or whether she was bathing in the nude. In any case, David should not be here at this time: he should be leading his army into war.

> ... it is clear from her actions that Bathsheba is both faithful to Uriah and obedient to the law.

It is David who takes the initiative to invite Bathsheba to the palace. First of all, he needs to find out who she is. His servants clearly inform him that she is the wife of Uriah, thus making him fully aware of the situation, and perhaps, in so doing, seek to discourage him from an act of adultery. However, in spite of this knowledge, David proceeds. When emissaries of the king arrive to bring her to the palace, Bathsheba can hardly refuse. As a woman of inferior social standing, she has little choice but to obey. The fact that she leaves the palace immediately after the act suggests that David is certainly not interested in a prolonged relationship with her.

On learning that Bathsheba is pregnant, David hatches a deathly plot. On the pretext of wanting to hear news of the campaign, he brings Uriah back home from the war. He invites him twice to the palace, the first time showering him with gifts, and the second time getting him drunk, hoping each time that Uriah will go home afterwards and lie with his wife. Then, when David learns that his plot has failed, he orders Uriah to be positioned on the battle field in a place where he will surely be killed. As if this were not enough, David then lies to cover up the fact. By the time we reach this point in the story, David is not only an adulterer—a thief of another man's wife—but also a murderer and a liar.

In contrast to king David who abuses the power invested in him, Uriah the outsider is faithful both to the Law of Moses and to the people of Israel. At the beginning of this story, Uriah is absent: he has gone into battle with all of Israel. The law forbade a man to have sexual relations with his wife during a time of war and Uriah is wholly faithful to his duty. Even when showered with gifts or totally drunk, he still refuses to go to bed with his wife. He eventually leaves Jerusalem again for the battlefield and there, tragically, he is killed believing that he is doing his duty for the nation.

Even if the passage does not directly speak of it, it is clear from her actions that Bathsheba is both faithful to Uriah and obedient to the law. When David sets eyes on her as she bathes on her balcony, she is not engaged in an act of exhibitionism, but on the contrary, is purifying herself following the commandments of the law—and she, the wife of a Gentile!

Once the pregnant Bathsheba learns that her husband Uriah is dead, she mourns her husband. Far from rejoicing in her liberation and congratulating herself on her availability to be married by the king, she shows herself to be faithful both to her husband and to the Law of Moses.

Just as she shares, as the wife of Uriah, in the righteousness of her first husband, so Bathsheba, as the wife of David, shares in punishment of her second husband. The child dies. At this point, David "consoles her". This is the first time that David demonstrates any real faithfulness or loving kindness towards her. She gives birth to a second child who is pleasing to God. Named "Beloved of God", this child survives.

This story points in the same direction as the other three that we have considered in this chapter. As king of Israel, David should have been the most righteous of all. However, he turns out to be nothing short of unfaithful, adulterous and murderous, abusing his power at every turn of the narrative. Meanwhile, the woman in the story is presented in many ways as a victim. She nonetheless remains faithful both to her first husband and then to her second. She not only becomes the means whereby David begins to repent of his sin, but also assures the family line, which will lead to the birth of the Messiah. After the death of the first baby, the text no longer speaks of 'She of Uriah', but calls Bathsheba by her own name.

Given that by the time Solomon is born, the writer refers to Bathsheba in this way, we might well expect to find the name Bathsheba in the genealogy of Matthew. But surprisingly, it is not there. Instead Matthew uses the patriarchal term 'she of Uriah'. Why should Matthew not wish to forget Uriah and his wife? Uriah has absolutely no biological link whatever with Solomon and the line of inheritance.

It may be that Matthew wants to remind his readers of David's sinfulness, and the punishment meted out on the following generations, lifted only at the birth of the Messiah.

It may be that Matthew wants to lay his emphasis on the forgiveness of God, which leads to the birth of Solomon. Alternatively, it may well be that Matthew is inviting us to reflect on the significance of the life of Uriah for the birth of Solomon. Uriah is killed as a result of the wickedness of David and his abuse of power. He dies on a battlefield where David himself might have lost his life had he shown more faithfulness to God and to the nation. The portrait we have of Uriah is of a just, faithful and righteous man before God who dies innocent of any crime. Perhaps Matthew refers to him in his genealogy because he gently prefigures the death of Jesus at the hands of wicked men who abuse of their power and condemn a wholly innocent man, the Son of God. At the moment when Jesus is condemned, Pilate's wife, whose insight we noticed in Chapter I, recognises in Jesus the presence of a just man. She does not fully understand the import of her words,

> *While he was sitting on the judgment seat, his wife sent word to him, "Have nothing to do with that innocent man, for today I have suffered a great deal because of a dream about him" (Matt. 27:19).*

Because of the innocent death of Uriah, a just and righteous man, David is enabled to marry Bathsheba, who gives birth to Solomon and assures the line of the Messiah. Even in such a complex knot of unsavoury, not to say criminal, action, the values of the Kingdom, hidden behind the adulterous and murderous action of the king, are still present in the lives of the ones Matthew wants to name in his genealogy.

The Remaining Question

So, why does Matthew insert the names of these four foreign women in his genealogy? We have already seen that these women, as outsiders, remind us of the infinite scope of the Kingdom of God. But we are now able to go further than this.

An initial interpretation of these stories might lead us to affirm that the genealogy contains the promise of God's forgiveness: if Jesus' ancestors led such scandalous lives, it is sure and certain proof that God brings hope to birth out of human sinfulness. In his great goodness and generosity at work in the worst of human wickedness, the miracle of the love of God is there. This would undoubtedly be a wholly and theologically Christian response: God who forgives brings life out of death.

Such an interpretation does not give full value to the hidden nature of the Kingdom. A more careful reading of these passages allows us to come to a richer understanding. Constrained by the cultures of their times, these women whom Matthew names in the genealogy were pushed by their circumstances into kinds of extreme behaviour, which down the centuries have attracted both censure and caricature. However, in one way or another they each demonstrate in complicated and morally ambiguous situations the values of the Kingdom of God, however hidden they might be by the unfaithfulness and wickedness of those around them. Even in writing his genealogy, Matthew invites his readers to "seek first the Kingdom of God" that is present beneath the surface in the lives of these women. Even in the worst excesses of the story of God's people, behind the labels, the yeast of the Kingdom is already present.

Mary, the Mother of Jesus: Unmarried Mother (Matt. 1:16; 18–25)

We now come in the genealogy to the name of Mary, the mother of Jesus. We might well decide to start as we have done with the other women in this chapter: with a superficial and scandalous resumé of the story. Only ... in Mary's case we do not really need to, because Matthew already does it for us. Inferring that Joseph initially assumes that Mary has behaved scandalously, Matthew explains that when Joseph learns of Mary's pregnancy, he decides to repudiate her in secret. It is quite clear that Joseph imagines that she has become pregnant by another man. At that time, a young woman who became pregnant outside of marriage or of the promise of it, became immediately unmarriageable. She destroyed the reputation of her own family and endangered the reputation of her betrothed and his family also.

Matthew announces that Joseph is a just man. We have already become familiar with this term, which carries huge significance the whole Gospel through. The appearance of this word tells us that Joseph is a man of the Kingdom. First, he takes the decision not to repudiate Mary in public and spares the two families the scandal that would arise from it. However, his thinking is interrupted by the word of God, which comes to him in a dream and allows him to see in Mary not the presence of doubtful morality, but the action of the Holy Spirit.

But just when he had resolved to do this, an angel of the Lord appeared to him in a dream and said, "Joseph, son of David, do not be afraid to take Mary as your wife, for the child conceived in her is from the Holy Spirit." (Matt. 1:20).

It is very striking that in contrast to Luke, who recounts the birth of Jesus far more from the point of view of Mary, Matthew is principally interested here in Joseph, Mary's pregnancy, and the birth of Jesus are presented essentially from his point of view. The righteousness of this good man has prepared him to listen faithfully to the word of the angel and consequently to recognise in Mary the presence of the Kingdom of God, which he would be unable to discern on his own. In order to see beneath the surface, to understand the action of God and to react to Mary in accordance with the will of God, Joseph needs divine wisdom and guidance.

The world in which we live can often seem to be very far from the ways of God. Violence can break out in our midst at any moment. Following a terrorist attack, fear can understandably imprison us in a distrust of others. We start to see others only at the most superficial level: we imagine we see a radicalised terrorist in every middle-eastern face, or a right-wing murderer in the features of a young person with fair hair and skin. Superficiality, often fuelled by internet communication, becomes a way of life. We lose the ability to welcome others with warmth and openness. We fear to deepen our relationships with others, or to take time building new friendships with neighbours or colleagues.

Throughout Matthew's Gospel, we are reminded of the dangers of labels and superficial judgments that can blind us to the truth within others. It is not only Joseph who is in danger of misunderstanding the action of God. Matthew tells how again and again, the presence of the Kingdom of God is not recognised, even when it is present in Jesus himself. The Jewish authorities see in Jesus the action of the devil (Matt. 12:24), while the people of Nazareth no longer believe in him (Matt. 13:57). Those who celebrate and welcome Jesus at his entry into Jerusalem see in him a military liberator rather than the one who expresses the love and sacrifice that lie at the heart of the Kingdom. They rapidly turn against him and bay for his blood. Meanwhile, those who condemn him to death are wholly and self-righteously persuaded that he is a blasphemer. The whole Gospel story warns us against the dangers of judging according to human values. If we do, we are in danger of aligning ourselves with the enemies of God.

In speaking of Joseph, Matthew reminds his readers that we need the Word of God and the discernment that comes from God if we are to cross the boundaries created by appearance and superficial expectation and seek the presence of the yeast of the Kingdom at work. As we worship, we learn to recognise the presence of the Kingdom manifest in Jesus. When we rise from worship, we need the humility and wisdom to seek the Kingdom at work in others as in ourselves, lurking even in the most unexpected places or hidden in the darkest corners.

Jesus says, "Seek first the Kingdom of God" (Matt. 6:33, ESV). In the course of the chapters that follow, we are going to seek the Kingdom, in the image of the yeast, active in the lives of the women who appear in the Gospel and in their relationship with Jesus. Each one, transformed by her encounter with him, is unique in one way or another and becomes a missionary, a passionate ambassador of the Kingdom in the place where God has set her. In learning to seek the values of the Kingdom in these passages, we pray that God will enable us to seek them in our everyday lives and become passionate and faithful agents of the Kingdom, growing in the likeness of Christ.

3 SERVING OTHERS: THE HUMBLE KINGDOM

But in the sight of Infinite Wisdom, believe me, there is more value in a little study of humility and in a single act of it than in all the knowledge in the world.
Teresa of Avila[14]

And so, whether we're answering the telephone all day, or working in the kitchen, or sitting at a typewriter, or slaving in a workshop, we will not wait for a change of occupation or lifestyle, or to be seized by a sudden extraordinary sense of conviction, before offering our arms and our hands and our mind to the spirit of Christ, so that through us he may continue to love. We need to do nothing more than this.
Madeleine Delbrêl[15]

When I watch someone making bread, I am always struck by the dynamism of their movements. There is such rhythm in kneading dough. First, the baker grabs a handful of dough and pulls it upwards. Then, with great energy, she plunges it down before taking another handful of dough from another edge and repeating the action all over again. If anyone were to keep their eye upon a single patch of the mixture, they might see it being lifted up, then brought down and lifted up again, only to be

---

14   (1515–1582), Spanish Carmelite, Doctor of the Church.
15   (1904–1964), French social worker and activist, writer, poet and founder of lay communities.

pummelled down once more, this time to an even lower place. In order to do its work, the yeast does not stay on the surface but is caught up in this extraordinary rhythm of movement from top to bottom, guided by the hand of the baker.

We tend to think of our lives in terms of a continuous progression that invites us to travel not from top to bottom but from the bottom to the top. As children, we think of growing up into adults. Once we have attained adulthood, society expects us to continue growing: not physically, but financially or sociologically, and, of course, in terms of our skills and abilities. In many parts of the world, the normal pattern of life is considered to be one in which we reach ever higher and higher until one day, some years later, we reach a senior place at work, or come to be so respected by the local community that we rub shoulders with other significant people. According to this way of thinking, living well is a matter of striving to reach a point in life where one can be honoured for what one has achieved, especially if one has come from a humble background.

The Kingdom of God, however, invites us to think in the opposite direction. Instead of growing up, rising towards a superior position, Jesus, the servant of God, rather humbled himself more and more,

> *who, though he was in the form of God,*
> *did not regard equality with God*
> *as something to be exploited,*
> *but emptied himself,*
> *taking the form of a slave,*
> *being born in human likeness.*
> *And being found in human form,*
> *he humbled himself*
> *and became obedient to the point of death—*
> *even death on a cross. (Phil. 2:6–8).*

The mysterious ways of the Kingdom of God never follow the patterns of human thinking. In the Kingdom, we are invited to move in the opposite direction. The more mature we grow in faith, the less status we are to seek for ourselves, and the humbler we are to learn to be.

> *"Whoever wants to be first must be last of all and servant of all" (Mark 9:35).*

> *Do nothing from selfish ambition or conceit, but in humility regard others as better than yourselves (Phil. 2:3).*

> *For my thoughts are not your thoughts,*
> *nor are your ways my ways, says the Lord (Is. 55:8).*

Peter's Mother-in-Law (Matt. 8:14–15)

I always find Matthew's picture of Peter's mother-in-law both touching and immensely challenging. It is such a short story that, occupying only a couple of verses, it is easily missed if the reader skims through it too quickly. However, these few verses are absolutely packed with wisdom and spiritual insight to help us understand the nature of God's Kingdom and our role within it. Matthew writes,

> *When Jesus entered Peter's house, he saw his mother-in-law lying in bed with a fever; he touched her hand, and the fever left her, and she got up and began to serve him (Matt. 8:14–15).*

At the moment when we meet this woman, she is lying ill, suffering from a fever. We are not told what she was suffering from, but at the time, any fever was dangerous for an older person, and given that this woman was already the mother-in-law of a grown man, she would have already have been considered to be well on in years in that present context.

If we were to cast a very superficial glance across this passage, we might understand the passage to be something like this,

> Peter's mother-in-law is ill. Lying with a fever, she is much too weak to do the housework or to get meals ready. The miraculous healing that Jesus performs enables her to rise immediately and resume her household duties. She serves a meal to Jesus. Everything returns to normal. Her life goes back to how it was before.

However, if we read this text a little more closely, seeking within it the powerful signs of the Kingdom of God, we might be excited to find evidence of the yeast at work in the life of this woman. To aid our thinking, we shall also be reflecting on the life of the English social worker, Sabina Bell.

Becoming a Servant of the Kingdom of God

Healed on the Inside

It is significant that Jesus is invited into the recesses of Peter's house. In the first century, houses in Mediterranean countries were, for the most part, constructed around a courtyard that was open to the street. Passers-by could walk in. The rooms towards the front of the house faced onto the street and often served as workshops or shops. Further on, there was the dining room that could be accessed from the street, living quarters, and even further inside, the women's quarters and those of the slaves.[16] If Jesus sees Peter's mother-in-law sick and lying

---
16   Carolyn Osiek and David L. Balch, *Families in the New Testament*

down, the implication is that he has been invited into the recesses of the house in order to heal her.

This is much more than an architectural detail. When Matthew tells us that Jesus enters the house where Peter's mother-in-law lies sick, he suggests that the healing he brings has to happen on the inside—of a person or of a group of people. There is no place beyond the reach of the transformative power of the Kingdom, not even the deepest recesses of the human heart.

These days we talk a very great deal about the possibilities of change. We instinctively sense that our lives could be different from how they are and we long for the opportunity to live, think and feel differently. We are all too easily seduced by the voices that would have us believe that by changing what is superficial, we will change our very lives. We only have to have a new hairstyle, a new sofa or a new address and, hey presto! We will feel entirely different—less lonely, more confident or be more admired by those around us. Advertisements for fashion, makeup or décor are often built on the same seductive messages. They try to convince us that new life can be simply bought along with a new product.

Very often the same scenario occurs at a political level. Those who stand for election, or come in other ways to power, promise that everything will suddenly be different with a change of leadership. They herald the arrival of a new dawn: corruption will cease, the gap dividing rich and poor will be eradicated and nothing will ever be the same again. Without question, it is true that certain outstanding leaders do indeed bring about huge, positive changes for their people. However, all too often, those who believe the words of their incoming leaders have their high hopes dashed.

Jesus cautions against such seductive and superficial

World: Households and House Churches (Louisville, KY: Westminster John Knox Press, 1997), p. 6.

ways of thinking. He warns his followers against giving too much attention to what they eat or wear,

> "Therefore do not worry, saying, 'What will we eat?' or 'What will we drink?' or 'What will we wear?' [...] But strive first for the kingdom of God and his righteousness, and all these things will be given to you as well." (Matt. 6:31, 33).

He warns the Pharisees against the dangers of cleaning "the outside of the cup and of the plate" and leaving "the inside full of greed and self-indulgence" (Matt. 23:25). He reminds them that appearance and reality are very different things, "So you also on the outside look righteous to others, but inside you are full of hypocrisy and lawlessness" (Matt. 23:28).

What is superficial cannot offer true transformation. Our lives can only be truly changed when we are touched by Christ in the very core, at the very depths of our being. At moments of terrible crisis, we can often feel as if we are walking through the valley of the shadow of death, not unlike Peter's mother-in-law. It can relate to times in our life when we are ill, bereaved or unemployed, or at moments of conflict in the family or at work. Sometimes it might be a national or political crisis that leaves us distressed and deeply fearful of the future. As individuals, as organisations or as a whole society, we can feel paralysed, blocked, incapable of carrying on normally or unable to take pleasure in the activities of our daily activities.

At such times of trial, it is very easy to imagine that it is always the others who need to change—in the way they think or in the ways they behave. However, it is for each one of us to recognise before God that we all need to be personally healed and transformed deep inside. Sometimes we are scared of such a thing: we are too proud, or we feel too guilty, or we are fearful of the change that Christ might bring. In order to allow Christ to come to us and touch us, we need the kind of humility displayed by the Peter's mother-in-law when she allows Jesus to approach her. The Kingdom of God—like the yeast that needs to be brought low in the mixture—is already at work in her.

A New Focus

The very moment when Jesus touches her, she gets up. In one sense, the evangelist is describing a perfectly normal, habitual, daily action: the woman gets up from her bed. However, the word that Matthew uses here to describe the action of the woman is used elsewhere in the New Testament to speak of the resurrection. Jesus uses the same word when he speaks about the Son of Man,

> *"The Son of Man is going to be betrayed into human hands, and they will kill him, and on the third day he will be **raised**" (Matt. 17:22–23).*

The angel at the tomb also uses the word,

> *"I know that you are looking for Jesus who was crucified. He is not here; for he **has been raised**, as he said" (Matt. 28:5–6).*

The word is not uniquely used for the resurrection of Jesus: it is also used to speak of those who follow him. In the letter to the Romans, the word appears again, not only to refer to the resurrection of Christ, but also in relation to the resurrection life that we share with him as those who are baptised,

> *Therefore we have been buried with him by baptism into death, so that, just as Christ was **raised** from the*

dead by the glory of the Father, so we too might walk in
newness of life *(Rom. 6:4).*

In using this particular word to describe the action of Peter's mother-in-law rising from a couch, Matthew underlines the essential truth of the Gospel that we see in Jesus Christ, crucified and risen: God brings new, resurrection life out of death. Matthew invites us to see in the action of the woman who gets up, the promise of the new life that is offered in him to all of us who allow ourselves to be touched by his life-giving power.

The Kingdom in the Everyday

Once she is up, the woman starts to serve. In the past, biblical scholars have explained her action by supposing that she serves a meal. After all, the preparation and service of meals for the family formed part of the daily duties of a woman in many households. The fact that Peter's mother-in-law is strong enough to serve a meal is proof that she was wholly healed. However, Matthew is careful to explain that it is not just a meal served to any one: this woman gets up and serves Jesus. There is action here. She directs her usual, practical, external life towards him. Her everyday activity is given a new focus: in the Kingdom of God our outward life is the expression of an internal, godly reality, which overflows from the inside into the activities of our daily living.

The *immediate* action of the woman in rising to serve Jesus offers us an important spiritual insight. The new life that God offers to us in Christ prepares and strengthens us for an active life as a citizen of the Kingdom from the very first moment. There is no time to lose. Touched by the hand of Christ and filled with God's new life, we each become an immediate witness and an ambassador of the Kingdom, in the very place where God has placed us. We do not have to wait for circumstances to be different, to have gained more confidence or to have reached a more advanced level of spiritual understanding.

For many years, I worked as a chaplain to a psychiatric hospital in Wales. I particularly remember the ward for elderly people with dementia. The ward sister, a very competent Christian woman in her middle years was a woman of extraordinary qualities. There were undoubtedly elements of her work that were far from easy: she had to deal with conflicts amongst the staff, with the distressed or sometimes indifferent families of the patients, not to mention the challenges represented by a limited budget. She needed to manage it all with wisdom and flexibility. I will always remember her as a wonderful and passionate ambassador of the Kingdom of God. While she did certain tasks in the corridors, it was her wont to sing old Welsh hymns. It was a marvellous idea. The melodies were often familiar to the elderly patients and even those who could no longer speak were still able to sing along.

> ... she explained that now she understood her work on the ward as a gift from God, as a calling to offer herself in service to the patients as to the Lord.

I remember one particular day when her voice resounded down the corridor and into the day-room where many of the patients were seated. "Let's dance!" She put on a recording of old dance tunes and took the hands of a patient beside her. His eyes were sparkling brightly. Other nurses and ward personnel did the same. Those patients who could no longer get to their feet started to move their arms about. Soon, everyone was dancing, and for just a few moments there was no longer a distinction between the healthy and the sick, between the strong and the weak, or between those rich in mental abilities and those who were poor. Everybody was part of the dance, celebrating together. What a wonderful foretaste of the Kingdom!

The next day I had the opportunity to speak to the ward sister. She told me that for many years, she had looked after her own mother who was suffering from Alzheimer's disease, and that she saw in the face of every patient on the ward the reflection of her own loved one. God had been at work within her, healing her grief, and with moving simplicity she explained that now she understood her work on the ward as a gift from God, as a calling to offer herself in service to the patients as to the Lord. I never found out if her particular way of doing her job was ever questioned, but I recognised in her the presence of the Kingdom of God, overflowing from within her to transform the daily life of the hospital.

The Call to Serve

The language of this tiny passage has even deeper meaning again. The call to serve lies at the heart of Jesus' message and the verb 'to serve' is a key word for the Kingdom of God. "Whoever wishes to be great among you," he says, "must be your servant" (Matt. 20:26–27).

All who follow Jesus, both men and women, are called to become as servants—as slaves. This would have sounded very shocking to Jesus' fellow Jews. God had delivered their people from slavery in Egypt—why would they put themselves voluntarily in the role of a slave?

The teaching of Jesus about servanthood was revolutionary, however, at another level. In the ancient world, and including in the culture of which Jesus was a part, the essential building block of society was the patriarchal, extended family household, founded on an arrangement of authority and submission. According to this system, an unmarried daughter was subservient to her father, a wife to her husband, and a widow to her sons or brother. Servants and slaves within the household were also under the authority of its head.

When Jesus leaves his family to exercise his ministry, he symbolically leaves behind him the structure of the patriarchal family and embraces a new quality of relationship in which all—both men and women—become the servants of others. When he calls men and women to follow him, he invites them to do the same. This presents a huge challenge both to men and to women. For men who, in the society of Jesus' day, were accustomed to being served, the teaching of Jesus represents a categorical change of thinking and lifestyle. They are being asked to leave behind ingrained, traditional ways of relating to others in order to belong to the new community of those who follow in the footsteps of the Son of Man who "came not to be served but to serve" (Matt. 20:28).

The same teaching of Jesus represents an equal change of thinking for women. They are called by Jesus to a life of servanthood, *not because they are women*, but because they are *disciples* of Jesus, following in his footsteps. They still live out their servanthood but in a wholly different context, in which they stand side by side with male disciples of Christ who are equally called to be servants. A new community of reciprocally serving relationships comes into being. The servanthood demonstrated by female followers of Jesus becomes an example not just for other women to imitate, but for all of Jesus' followers, both men and women.

When Peter's mother-in-law rises to serve Jesus, she becomes an example for the whole Christian community. Her service to Jesus is not the traditional act of a woman towards a man, but the act of a true disciple following in the footsteps of the one who demonstrates the divine nature of true service. She is an imitator of Christ. She has a new point of orientation, and becomes fully a citizen of the Kingdom of God. This little story about Peter's mother-in-law thus offers us an illustration of God's intention for us all: to touch us, renew us and equip us for a life of service at the very heart of the Kingdom.

Deepening our Life of Service

Sabina Bell
Service Inside and Outside of the Church

Not long ago I was attending the funeral of Sabina Bell, a Christian woman who, throughout her life, had given herself to service. She had been a deacon in the church in which I had grown up and I had known her from my earliest childhood. I had stayed in contact with her all through my student years and during my pastorates in the South-West and in Wales, and we were still in contact not long before she died at the grand old age of 96. She was one of those exceptional Christians who had the capacity to take care of everyone in the church. If there was someone in distress, it was she who went to visit them and had the right words to say. If there was a conflict between individuals, she seemed to know how to pour oil on troubled water. If someone left the church under the disapproving eye of certain of its members, it was she who would still be in contact with them twenty years later.

When in my teens, I was being prepared to receive believer's baptism, she was appointed by the church meeting to be one of my 'visitors': a spiritual companion and friend. I remain grateful to God for the wisdom of the church meeting in appointing her. She accompanied me faithfully during the weeks of preparation. Then on the day of my baptism, I received a card from her with a letter inside it. In the letter, she encouraged me to stay faithful to the Christian Church, even in the times when it failed to live up to its true calling to be a witness to Christ. She urged me to stay always hopeful. Then her letter passed to the theme of service. As disciples of Christ we were called into God's service all the days of our life, she reminded me. Yes, we were called to serve Christ in the Church. But we were never to forget that we were also called to serve him just as much, if not more, outside of the Church.

I remember that at the time, I was deeply struck by these words. Somehow and from somewhere I had absorbed the idea that Christian service was something that was principally expressed by participating in the life of the Christian community, through faithful attendance at communion, through regular presence at church meetings, and through regular giving and prayer for other members of the fellowship. Indeed, the secretary of the church had written to me only the week before confirming as much.

But then, Sabina had a deeper and wider vision. She helped me understand that Christian service goes much further than the boundaries of the local church community, and is to be expressed in every walk of life. Sabina believed passionately that Christian witness needed to extend to the furthest corners of the earth.

As a teenager, Sabina had been forced to give up her studies as her parents did not have the means to pay for her to go further. She would have loved to have been a nurse, but she did not have the necessary qualifications to allow her access to the training. Finally, she found a job in a hospital, working as a librarian, setting up a library for the patients from nothing. After that, she became a receptionist in a psychiatric hospital where she learnt to serve those whom she understood to be amongst the most excluded from society. When I reflect on her life, it seems to me that at each stage of her life, God was preparing her for the next one.

As a young woman, she was still living with her parents when Alfred Bell arrived to be the new minister of their church. He needed accommodation, and Sabina's parents offered him a room in their house. Alfred and Sabina fell in love and Sabina found herself with a whole new life opening up before her as the wife of a minister. Down the years, she accompanied her husband and together their pastoral gifts were recognised by all. They both had a sense of service that went beyond the horizon of the church members. During the war years, they supported people who were grieving and traumatised. The more they gave themselves in service, the more they realised how many needs surrounded them.

They organised a series of meetings in the church where they invited people who were serving in the community to come and talk about their work or their particular ministry. A great moment arrived the day they heard someone speak about a home for young people with physical disabilities. At the time, people who needed a wheelchair often lived rather shut away in specialised accommodation, but the person who came to speak talked about a new approach, where the home endeavoured to integrate their residents much more into the community. The organisation was looking for a new director and approached Alfred and Sabina.

It was an important moment for them. Up to this point, their Christian service had revolved principally around the life of the church. Perhaps they had imagined that one day they would move on to a ministry in another church setting—perhaps in a larger or more well-known church. But now, they were asked to re-examine these assumptions and grapple with the idea of working in a context that might turn out to be much more challenging. After a time of prayer and discernment, they accepted. Alfred left his ministerial post in order to take up the new role.

They arrived at the centre to discover that it was beset with significant financial challenges. Sabina offered to work in a voluntary capacity as a social worker, acknowledging that she had no professional qualifications or experience as a social worker. The board agreed. A year later, when the financial situation had recovered, she was offered the permanent post, such were the gifts and skills she had shown. She continued to work there until her retirement.[17]

Looking back on her life, it seems to me that she could well have thought that she had already reached the pinnacle of a spiritual call as a minister's wife. Very often testimonies are told in a way that suggests that we have reached the high point of a call from God when we exercise a particular ministry *in* the Church. But the journey that Sabina was called to make reminds us that God's ways are often much wider and more profound. The Kingdom of God does not close us down, but opens us up to the wider community. Sabina's ministry in the context of the church served only to prepare her for the work that God had in store for her in the most hidden corners of society. She had learnt so much in the Church: to love others,

---

17   Geoffrey Ottaway's sermon preached at Sabina Bell's funeral, 2015, unpublished.

to have compassion, to listen to others, to understand the precious nature of each human being in the eyes of God—and so much more besides. But it was only a preparatory stage. God was leading her into a context outside of the Church where she would need to dig spiritually deep and put into practice everything that she had learnt before.

The Church: The School of the Kingdom

I often wonder how much our understanding of service would grow if we were to consider the Church as a school of service, rather than as the principal context of its expression. Everything that we did in the service of brothers and sisters in the church would then be like an apprenticeship that would prepare us for Christian service in a wider context. Church would be a training ground in which we would be exhorted and encouraged, not to mention corrected when need be. It would be the place in which, as beginners, we made our worst mistakes. In church, we would learn and gain experience that would strengthen us and equip us for a greater sphere of service elsewhere. After all, the word 'disciple' means 'pupil'. As disciples of Christ we are pupils in the school of God's love, and the Church is our classroom.

When Jesus speaks of serving, he does not limit his ministry to certain contexts. His ministry as the obedient servant of God expresses itself at every moment of his life and leads him to the cross. For Jesus, there is not a 'spiritual' context that is cut off from any other. His service, as an expression of the love of God, is part and parcel of his whole being. For those who follow Jesus, there is no question of being more of a servant in one place than another. God calls us to serve in our every activity and in every place: at work, at home, in our leisure activities, in social and political contexts just as much as in the church.

Sabina Bell (cont'd)

Alfred and Sabina became members of their local Baptist church. As a social worker, Sabina remained in the 'school' of the Church and continued to serve there as a deacon. It was here that I came to know her. For her, every place belonged to God. There were no boundaries in Christian service. As far as she was concerned, God had entrusted her with the care of the residents of the home just as much as he had entrusted her with the care of the church members. Receiving her work as a gift from the hand of God, she believed that her ministry in the home was blessed and directed by him.

At the end of her life, Sabina became disabled herself and needed a wheelchair. She had a weak heart and was unable to undergo the operation that might have increased her mobility. Widowed by now for quite some years, she was thankful to move into a home, where she found herself surrounded by other residents, young and old, many of whom also were in a wheelchair. In her nineties, she still was not tired of serving others. From the quietness of her room, she continued to exercise a ministry of prayer and friendship on the telephone, always ready to listen and share the burden of another in distress.

In the next-door room, there was a young man who had been paralysed as a result of a car accident. He had no movement in his arms and legs. He no doubt reminded her of some of the young people she had once worked with. Sabina knew that he was an ardent supporter of Arsenal football team and that he was devastated no longer to be able to attend matches. Having learnt in the Church—in the school of the Kingdom—of the importance of speaking for those with no voice, she wrote secretly to the manager explaining the young man's situation and asking if they would allow the young man, plus a carer, to attend the match. We may never know exactly what she wrote in the letter, but can imagine her delight when she eventually received a reply saying that they would be delighted to help, and would not charge for the tickets.[18] When she went into a care home, Sabina could have rested on her laurels and said to herself that her years of Christian service were over. However, despite her physical fragility, she continued to serve. She just could not help it. As a woman of the Kingdom, she had learnt to see the world from the point of view of the humblest and the poorest of the earth, and the yeast of the Kingdom was at work in her right to the very end.

On the day that she was baptised as a believer, Sabina could not have known that she would end up working amongst people with special needs. None of us knows where the path of our faith will lead. But we do know that in following Christ, we are walking on the road of service in the Kingdom of God. Such a road never promises riches or success. On the contrary, it is likely to lead us more and more towards humility, and towards the hidden places of the earth that are as poor as they are bringers of joy, a long way from the point from which we started.

The Values of the World and the Values of the Kingdom

However small it may be, the action of the woman in our Bible passage for this chapter is drawn across the social and po-

---
18   Hilary Alexander's address given at Sabina Bell's funeral, 2015, unpublished.

litical canvas of the first century world. We have already seen how the service of Peter's mother-in-law belongs fully to the life of the Kingdom. When we read her story in the context of the Gospel story as a whole, we begin to understand how much her action stands totally in contrast to the abuses of power demonstrated by some of the other characters in the Gospel story.

As his Gospel progresses, Matthew alludes to acts of injustice and violence committed by those who oppress the poorest people in order to bolster their own power and reputation, and it is not very difficult to see in such portraits the reflection of the troubles of our own world. The Gospel writer never shrinks from telling of human kingdoms that are often the enemies of God's Kingdom (Matt. 10:18) and of corrupt kings who murder their own people (Matt. 2:16) and have prophets who speak truth to them put to death (Matt. 14:3–4; 10). Matthew tells not only of corrupt kings and rulers but also of other authorities within society who abuse their power. He describes the scribes and the Pharisees who are accused by Jesus of hypocrisy and of exploiting the most vulnerable in society. He points to those who amass wealth at the expense of the poorest people, leaving them to a life of poverty (Matt. 23:14). He also shows how the condemnation of Jesus comes as a result of the corruption of those in power, as they assemble and make plans to have him put to death (Matt. 26:3–40). Even the crowd becomes complicit in the violence (Matt. 27:26).

Jesus constantly reminds his disciples that there is no place in the Kingdom for those who express their self-seeking thirst for glory through acts of injustice and abuse of power. The followers of Jesus are called to resist being inveigled into the mentality of seeking the highest and most glorious place. On the contrary, those who walk in the footsteps of Jesus are invited to live in a different way: to consider the needs of others above their own, and to give themselves humbly to serve others.

> *But Jesus called them to him and said, "You know that the rulers of the Gentiles lord it over them, and their great ones are tyrants over them" (Matt. 20:25).*

When we return to the story of Peter's mother-in-law, we understand that in describing the action of a woman who rises, healed, to serve Jesus, Matthew presents us with someone who embodies the extraordinary values of the Kingdom, which both men and women are called to make known. Her spiritual mind-set is wholly different from that of other characters described in the background of the Gospel narrative. In contrast, even to the apostles who are shown later in the Gospel story to compete with one another for positions of honour in the Kingdom, this woman is true to Kingdom values.

Every one of our actions, however small it might be, is performed within a cultural context and written against a social and political background. Some actions have lesser significance, while others speak very powerfully of our moral choices and commitments. We are daily faced with important choices: shall we be conformed to the values and thinking of today's world, so eaten by prejudice and racism, fear and injustice? Or shall we remain faithful to the call humbly to serve others? The apostle Paul urges us,

> *Do not be conformed to this world, but be transformed by the renewing of your minds, so that you may discern what is the will of God—what is good and acceptable and perfect (Rom. 12:2).*

4 Reaching Out: The Welcoming Kingdom

Think what the world could look like if we took care of the poor even half as well as we do our Bibles!
Dorothy Day[19]

If the lonely and the frightened are to be comforted, it is our embrace, not God's, that will comfort them.
Dorothee Sölle[20]

Jesus' parable describes activity. Left all alone on the shelf, yeast is totally inactive. It does not do anything. As it grows older, it even loses its strength. However, once dissolved in water, yeast only needs to be incorporated into the flour for it to begin to act. At that moment, it becomes what it is designed to be: an extraordinary agent of transformation.

Flour is a substance whose qualities are wholly different from those of yeast. But if the yeast is to demonstrate its true nature, it needs to be completely mixed in with the flour. It demands vigour on the part of the baker and unwavering focus on the task at hand.

---

19 (1897–1980), American journalist, community builder, co-founder of the Catholic Worker.
20 (1929–2003), German theologian.

It is the same with the Kingdom of God. The Kingdom is not a precious substance that needs to be kept separate and protected from everything else. It is the dynamic catalyst for change that God mixes and incorporates into a myriad of different contexts in order to accomplish his transformative purpose.

It is intriguing that Jesus chooses yeast to describe the reign of God. In the story of the people of God, God's activity is often associated with the absence of yeast—the total opposite to what we have in the parable. The Israelites, for instance, are commanded to eat *un*leavened bread during the Passover,

> *This day shall be a day of remembrance for you. You shall celebrate it as a festival to the Lord; throughout your generations you shall observe it as a perpetual ordinance. Seven days you shall eat unleavened bread; on the first day you shall remove leaven from your houses, for whoever eats leavened bread from the first day until the seventh day shall be cut off from Israel (Ex. 12:14–5).*

In other parts of the New Testament, yeast serves as an image for impurity, and in these contexts, the yeast stands for all that is *contrary* to the purposes of God,

> *And he cautioned them, saying, "Watch out—beware of the yeast of the Pharisees and the yeast of Herod" (Mark 8:15).*

> *Meanwhile, when the crowd gathered by the thousands, so that they trampled on one another, he began to speak first to his disciples, "Beware of the yeast of the Pharisees, that is, their hypocrisy" (Luke 12:1).*

> *Clean out the old yeast so that you may be a new batch, as you really are unleavened. For our paschal lamb, Christ, has been sacrificed (1 Cor. 5:7).*

However, in his parable, Jesus uses the image of the yeast in an entirely *positive* sense. He uses it to speak not of sin or of human impurity, but of the activity of God. Yeast is something to be glad about, not something to be avoided. It is as if, in telling this parable, Jesus signals that he is saying something different, something new, and preparing his listeners to understand that their traditional ways of thinking are about to be challenged.

> *Is not this the fast that I choose:*
> *to loose the bonds of injustice,*
> *to undo the thongs of the yoke,*
> *to let the oppressed go free,*
> *and to break every yoke?*
> *Is it not to share your bread with the hungry,*
> *and bring the homeless poor into your house;*
> *when you see the naked, to cover them,*
> *and not to hide yourself from your own kin?*
> *(Is. 58:6–7).*

"There is nothing outside a person that by going in can defile, but the things that come out are what defile" (Mark 7:15).

How does God's love abide in anyone who has the world's goods and sees a brother or sister in need and yet refuses help? Little children, let us love, not in word or speech, but in truth and action (1 John 3:17–18).

The Woman with a Flow of Blood (Matt. 9:20–22)

This is one of the stories of women in Matthew's Gospel that I suspect has been a favourite amongst preachers of all kinds. As a young Christian, I really loved this story and used to return to it time and time again. At that stage in my life I found great inspiration in the story, which spoke to me of healing and faith. But I confess that as I grow older, this story increasingly challenges and perturbs me. It takes me right out of my comfort zone and invites me to call my attitudes towards others into question.

> *Then suddenly from behind him came a woman, who had been suffering from a haemorrhage for twelve years, and she touched the fringe of his cloak, for she was thinking, "If only I can touch his cloak I shall be saved." Jesus turned round and saw her; and he said to her, "Courage, my daughter, your faith has saved you." And from that moment the woman was saved. (Matt. 9:20–22, NJB).*

If we were simply to gloss over this passage, we might understand it rather like this,

> A woman has been suffering from a haemorrhage for many years. Excluded from society, she is victim to certain traditions which existed in the first century but which no longer hold society captive today. Fearful of being seen, she hides away in the crowd. The moment she touches Jesus, she is healed, and, calling her forward, Jesus congratulates her for her faith.

But what if we were to look at this text again, looking

more closely for the signs of the yeast of the Kingdom at work? How might our reading be deepened? Let us take a closer look at this remarkable and challenging narrative.

Fear of Touch and Isolation

Not unlike many of the other women who appear in this Gospel, this woman is anonymous. Matthew introduces her simply as 'a woman'. We do not know her name, or exactly where she came from. We know her only by her physical condition, one that determines and defines her relationship with men, not to say her relationship with the whole of society.

The woman has been suffering from the flow of blood for twelve long years. This number not only tells us the length of time that this woman has endured her suffering, but also has an important symbolic meaning. Twelve was the number of the tribes of Israel and the number of apostles called by Jesus. This number has a very Jewish resonance, and suggests that the woman's condition needs to be understood in relation to the Jewish law.

At the time of Jesus, the idea of purity controlled everyday relationships and defined the social boundaries upon which society was built. The people of God expressed their wholeness and their relationship with God by particular practices that were intended to safeguard the cultural and religious purity of the nation. These practices distinguished them from the other, Gentile, nations. For example, there were laws that governed which foods were eaten and how they were prepared; ones that dictated practices of washing; and others that controlled the contexts in which human contact could and could not take place.

The laws governing purity also specified that people with certain physical conditions were ritually unclean, such as those with a skin disease or women during their period.

According to these laws, a man could become unclean simply by touching such people, or by coming into contact with an object that they had touched.

As a result, the book of Leviticus contains laws that command a man to avoid all contact with a woman who was losing blood,

> When a woman has a discharge of blood that is her regular discharge from her body, she shall be in her impurity for seven days, and whoever touches her shall be unclean until the evening. Everything upon which she lies during her impurity shall be unclean; everything also upon which she sits shall be unclean. Whoever touches her bed shall wash his clothes, and bathe in water, and be unclean until the evening. Whoever touches anything upon which she sits shall wash his clothes, and bathe in water, and be unclean until the evening; whether it is the bed or anything upon which she sits, when he touches it he shall be unclean until the evening. If any man lies with her, and her impurity falls on him, he shall be unclean seven days; and every bed on which he lies shall be unclean.
>
> If a woman has a discharge of blood for many days, not at the time of her impurity, or if she has a discharge beyond the time of her impurity, all the days of the discharge she shall continue in uncleanness; as in the days of her impurity, she shall be unclean (Lev. 15:19–25).

It is striking how many times the words "touch" and "unclean" appear in this passage. The repetition of both words makes it clear that in matters of purity, the two ideas are deeply connected. Touch from a woman who is bleeding is a threat to purity and to be avoided by a man seeking to keep himself ritually clean at all costs.

This had a significant impact on daily life. The men of the household abstained from all contact with a female family member during her period and with all objects that she had touched. Usually, women had to live separately from the main house during this time in order to avoid all contact with objects that, in their turn, might 'contaminate' one of the men of the family.

When Matthew introduces the woman of our passage, he explains that she has been suffering from a flow of blood not just for a few days every month, but continuously for years. In all this time, she has been untouchable, someone to be rejected and avoided by righteous and respectable people.

The implications of this are far-reaching. The woman's condition has not only rendered her unclean, but has also made her unable to have children—in a time when it was thought that a woman's primary purpose was to bear children to her husband. Matthew tells us nothing about the family situation of this particular woman. However, such a condition might well have made a married woman vulnerable to rejection by her husband. Equally, it would have made an unmarried woman doubly unfit for marriage, which was the principal way a woman could both be provided for, and occupy what was considered to be her rightful place in society.

To top it all, this woman is forbidden from entering the women's courtyard in the Temple, which denied access to women with this condition. It is as though she has no place whatever among God's worshipping people. She is totally cut off from family and community, an outcast, entirely alone.

While our societies are, for the most part, no longer governed by written purity codes like these, there are still many people who, for a variety of reasons, get pushed to the very edges of our communities. Other people avoid them or give them a wide berth. At the beginning of my ministry I worked in a city in the South-West of England. One day in December, I was walking up the main street in front of the church. A young homeless man was sitting down in front of a shop window and I stopped to talk to him. He told me his name was Joe. He had fled from home to escape his violent father, who had recently been released from jail. As there was no way that he could be safe at home, he had run away and taken to the streets. After talking to him for a few minutes, I continued on my way.

Just a few weeks later, on Christmas Eve, I was in town again, and bumped into Joe as I was doing some last-minute shopping. "Joe," I said, "how are you?" To my great surprise, I saw tears welling up, and he started to cry. "Whatever's the matter?" I asked. Joe smiled at me through his tears. "You called me by my name. You remembered it!" The depth of his emotion suddenly opened my eyes to a reality I had not ever quite fully appreciated. How isolated, how lonely this young man was. I was so accustomed to others' calling me Mary that I never really thought about it. I simply took it for granted that they would do so. How very rich I was! Suddenly I realised the kind of isolation that existed just minutes away from the church. How many others like Joe must there be?

I continued my conversation with Joe, who told me that he would really like to come to midnight communion. He loved singing Christmas carols, he said, because it reminded him of his childhood. "But God doesn't want me," he added with sadness in his voice. "I drink too much. My life's messed up. And I'll get looks. They'll be thinking 'where did he crawl out from?'" Of course, I immediately tried to reassure this young man that God would never cut him off: God loves us and welcomes us all, regardless of how messed up our lives have become. But perhaps I was wrong not to share more of my thoughts with him. It seemed to me that this young man had more humility and more awareness of his need for forgiveness than plenty of others who would be in church later.

I repeated my invitation to Joe to come to worship later in the evening, assuring him once again that God's love extends to all. But in taking my leave of him I could not help but think about the other people who might be at the service. Perhaps Joe was right: there would certainly be those that were present who would be less than delighted to find themselves singing carols next to a young man who smelled of booze and sweat. They did not need to put their feelings into words: Joe could just guess what they were thinking. To make matters worse, he imagined that the judgment of others reflected the judgment of God. If others were avoiding him, he thought that God must be avoiding him too.

Hearing God's Challenge

Let us turn back for a moment to the story of the woman with the flow of blood. Perhaps she, too, feels exactly the same way as Joe did: judged by others because of her condition, and, by extension, judged by God too. For the past 12 years, she has had the capacity to render a man ritually impure by coming into contact with him. It would be totally understandable if, after all this time, this woman simply abandoned all hope of cure and hid herself away, resigned to bearing the 'unclean' label to the end of her days.

When we who live in a secular society read this passage at a distance of 2000 years, it is very easy to think that such ideas of separation and impurity no longer exist—after all, we have come a long way since then! However, Matthew's account of the woman with the flow of blood invites us to reflect on the ways in which our own fragmented world inflicts isolation on others by judging and avoiding them. The passage asks us to examine the ways we live alongside the widespread poverty of loneliness, both oblivious to it and untroubled by it.

I had the opportunity to do so after leaving the South-West, when I went to work as a minister in a small town in the Welsh valleys. In the past, it had been a very prosperous town, and large numbers of men had worked in the mines in the area. There had been a wonderful market twice a week that attracted people from villages further up the valleys. The older people in the church would reminisce about the lovely shops and boutiques that drew people even from Cardiff and other bigger towns. Those older people would also repeat the stories and memories of the Welsh revivals[21] that their parents and grandparents had handed down to them: churches bursting to the seams, powerful preachers and hymn-singing to raise the roof. Many churches had been built during that period: in our town, there were five church buildings in the main street, not to mention others in the surrounding areas.

By the time I settled there, however, many things had changed. The unemployment rate was worrying. The market had grown smaller, and many of the shops that managed to survive were those selling their wares at bargain prices. Meanwhile, the signs of revival had dwindled, not to say disappeared. Of the five church buildings in the main street, two were being used for other community purposes. The Christian churches often felt rather side-lined, aware of occupying a less important place in the community than in times gone by.

The local church of which I became the minister had always had a significant interest in Christian mission, offering financial and spiritual support to the work of missionaries in other parts of the world. It was a warm, down-to-earth and open-hearted sort of fellowship. It had welcomed pastors and students from faraway places, and had a strong, passionate commitment to issues of justice and peace. Meanwhile it

---

21   1735–1790, 1859 and 1904–1905. Revivals in different towns also took place: 1866, 1879, 1887, 1890 and 1892.

had a wonderful record of offering the numerous rooms in its premises for use by local community-building groups.

We began as a local church to sense that God was inviting us to serve our own community in a different way, and started to ask questions about local needs. Meanwhile, working together, Christians from a number of different local churches in the area became aware that there might be a small number of homeless people wandering the streets. On wet days, these homeless youngsters often sheltered in the subway that led into the centre of town.

The group from the churches brought forward a proposal that the churches of the town should work together to provide a night shelter. The group also proposed that the night shelter should take place on our premises, as we were the best situated geographically to offer a welcome. Our building was also probably the most suitable.

This was a big question. While some people in our local church were very enthusiastic, others, understandably, were far more cautious. Some feared that if we were to take this action, it would damage our good reputation in the town and that existing groups that used the premises would go elsewhere. Parents might not want to bring their children to the church. Others were very nervous that the spirituality and decorum of services might be undermined by the presence of people who were drunk or under the influence of drugs. And what would be the legal and insurance implications? As the word got around, I started to receive letters from members of the public. Most of them argued that there was no need to do this work because homelessness was not an issue in the town. It was a lovely place, and we should not spoil it by welcoming homeless people into it. Any people that really were homeless had only to move on to a larger city.

For us as Christians, there can be contacts that can make us uncomfortable. Yes, of course, we are in favour of others hearing the Gospel message and we want our churches to be full. At the same time, there can be some people from whom we prefer to steer clear. The manner in which we welcome certain groups or individuals can sometimes be less than warm, for fear of the way others might see us, or of appearing to compromise our Christian values, or for fear of that 'something' we are unable to articulate. Of course, we know only too well that there is nothing new in this: in the not too distant past so-called 'good' Christians were careful to avoid divorced people or children who had been born outside of wedlock. Single mothers often passed themselves off as widows in order to find a place in the Christian community. Certain churches would not welcome such people to their services or would not allow them to become members.

Even if attitudes have indeed evolved with time, the fear of impurity still exists. We can tell ourselves it would be better not to become too friendly with those whose lifestyles reflect values or cultures different from ours. We can choose to avoid the neighbour who is always drunk, or never stops swearing, and keep a safe distance from the artist with the bohemian lifestyle. We might muster a 'hello' in the street, but perhaps little else. Often, we prefer to develop close relationships with other Christians, and we can end up living in a kind of Christian cocoon, as if we believed that the more faithful we are to God, the more we need to keep ourselves apart.

God Welcomes and Includes

Thank God that his ways are not ours! If we are to take the parable seriously, we are mistaken if we think that the yeast of the Kingdom needs to be kept separate, on a shelf all by itself. If it were true that faithfulness to God demanded separateness from others, Jesus would never have been born. He would have stayed in heaven. In fact, Jesus demonstrates precisely the opposite: perfect love never seeks to push another away. Perfect love, which drives out fear, reaches out and offers welcome. It goes out of its way to seek the lost sheep, the lost coin, those on the margins of society, those who are rejected and excluded by others. The yeast of the Kingdom needs to be mixed in if it is to demonstrate its power.

The homeless people of our town were, in one way or another, those rejected by others, living on the edges of the community. One day when I was in town, I sat down to talk to a young man who was sheltering in the subway. A few minutes later, a woman who was walking by with an empty shopping bag spat at us. The church members had good reason to fear that the church might lose its respectable reputation if we were to start welcoming homeless people onto our premises.

Besides all these concerns, our church community was aware that if we were to go in this direction, we would be stepping out into territory we had never entered before. What we already were doing 'worked' well, in a sense, and there was a voice of reason that argued for not 'fixing' what was 'not broke'. We had no experience in this area, and few other churches, at this time, were engaged in this kind of ministry. We had no idea how things might develop, what difficulties we would have to face in the future, or what challenges we might have to confront.

Fearless Touch and Community

Let us return once again to the woman with the flow of blood. She is unclean according to the law and is, as a result, untouchable, isolated and lonely. But within her, the yeast of the Kingdom is already at work. Instead of remaining the same, programmed for death, she dares to believe that the reign of God extends to her and those like her: isolated, sick, poor, invisible. She understands that in the Kingdom, 'touch' works the other way around. Far from avoiding contact with people who are ritually unclean according to the Law, Jesus is ready to do the opposite. Without fear, he reaches out generously. He takes both Peter's mother-in-law (Matt. 8:15) and the daughter of the ruler (Matt. 9:25) by the hand. He touches the bier that is carrying the dead body of the young man he raises to life (Luke 7:15) and refuses to be scandalised when a woman washes his feet with her tears (Luke 7:36–50). By extending a loving touch or receiving it from others, he expresses welcome, not rejection, and offers healing.

In other Gospel stories, the individuals that Jesus heals through touch approach Jesus from the front. They usually fall down before him in reverence and humility, and implore him with words to heal them or the one they love. Jesus responds to such requests with compassion. He takes action and reaches out. The leper asks for healing in this way (Matt. 8:1–4), as do the two blind men (Matt. 9:27–30).

This woman, however, is a one-off, a bit of a revolutionary. It is as if she conducts an experiment in faith. First of all, instead of approaching Jesus from the front, as the ruler had done, she approaches him from *behind*. When the evangelist *Mark* tells this story, he includes in it the detail that the woman came up behind Jesus *in the crowd*. Mark gently suggests thereby that the women is trying to find a way of remaining hidden. Interestingly, however, Matthew does not mention the crowd. This means that the emphasis in his telling of the story falls much more strongly on the woman's approach from behind. He highlights how very different she is compared to others whose stories he has told.

This is not the only way in which this woman is different. Without asking, she takes the initiative, reaches out and touches Jesus' garment. Unlike the synagogue ruler who falls down before Jesus and begs him to come and heal his daughter (Matt. 9:18), she does not ask, or beseech, or implore or beg.

She simply *acts*. She has the courage and the consciousness of another reality, manifest in Jesus, in which isolation is overturned by love and uncleanness is overcome by touch. She simply puts her faith into practice. Contrary to what the law commands, she goes ahead and ... *touches* him.

In the light of all this, we will not be in the least surprised to find that the word "touch" is repeated in this episode,

> *Then suddenly a woman who had been suffering from hemorrhages for twelve years came up behind him and **touched** the fringe of his cloak, for she said to herself, "If I only **touch** his cloak, I will be made well"* (Matt. 9:20–21).

In our contemporary situation in which we are acutely aware of the pressing need to safeguard children and vulnerable people, the whole area of 'touch' has become very problematic. At the time of writing, the coronavirus pandemic and the need for physical distancing has made us further wary, and rightly so, of the touch that can pass on disease and death. However, Matthew, telling the story of the woman for his own time, uses the word 'touch' in a wholly positive sense. He offers a deliberate contrast between the woman's isolation created by human fear, and the love of the Kingdom made known in Jesus. Whereas the purity codes in the book of Leviticus linked touch with the danger of ritual uncleanness, Matthew links touch with welcome, healing and well-being. Where fear of touch led to isolation, *fearless* touch will lead to community.

Let us not gloss over the significance of this woman's action too quickly. After all, it is she who touches *Jesus*, rather than the other way around. This is the biggest faith-experiment of all. Other figures in the Gospel wait for Jesus to say the word, to reach out, to place his fingers on their eyes or ears or mouth, or extend his hand and lift them from their bed. This woman dares to pre-empt the miracle by daring to do what Jesus himself does. In a way, she is like Peter who steps out onto the water (Matt. 14:29), seeking to walk on it like Jesus does. Yet, even Peter asks and waits for Jesus to give the command to come toward him before stepping out of the boat. This woman is amazingly independent. She waits for no confirmation other than that given by her own faith conviction. She instinctively knows that perfect love welcomes.

The confirmation of her act occurs afterwards, when she is healed and Jesus recognises her faith. The yeast of the Kingdom is active within her, and this woman of great stature in faith, becomes yet another in our series of women who powerfully herald the life of the Kingdom of God.

Back in Wales, the church of which I was minister needed creative faith not unlike that of the woman with the flow of blood. As a local church, we were faced with an important decision: whether to launch out in a way we had not tried before, and seek to offer a welcome to the most isolated and forgotten people of our town. Having prayed, listened and talked together, the church courageously took the step of opening its premises every night to those who might otherwise have to sleep in front of shop doorways. We would offer a meal in the evening, and would provide beds for a dozen sleepers and a breakfast in the morning. A local organisation working with homeless people provided staff for the night and greatly assisted us by offering professional experience, advice and expertise. We had a shower installed in the building. With the extraordinary help of many Christians from other local churches and that of members of the local community, we set up a rota of volunteers.

From the first day that the church opened its doors, we discovered the meaning of the word 'contact'! Socks of different colours and sizes were found dangling from the legs of stacked-up chairs. Toothbrushes suddenly appeared on the shelf reserved for Bibles and shoe laces—and worse—got lost behind the radiators. Young homeless people started occasionally to come to church and, it was true, they were often in a drunken state, or tired and cold and seeking warmth. At one evening service, during a time of silent prayer, the throaty rattle of deep and regular snoring emerged from a pew at the back of the church and echoed around the sanctuary, bringing a smile to the lips of not a few whose heads were bowed. On another occasion, as the elements of Holy Communion were being distributed, according to Baptist tradition, amongst the congregation in the pews, one hungry young man suddenly put his hand out, took the whole bread and rammed it ravenously into his mouth. Clearly, he had not eaten for days.

Knowing God's Saving Power

If we take the trouble to turn back to our Bible passage, we discover that the woman believes that if only she can manage to touch the edge of Jesus' robe, she will be saved. What might she mean by such a word? It appears three times altogether in our story in different forms, and suggests that for Matthew, being 'saved' is an important theme,

> *"If only I can touch his cloak I shall be **saved**." Jesus turned round and saw her; and he said to her, "Courage, my daughter, your faith has **saved** you." And from that moment the woman was **saved** (Matt. 9:20–22, NJB).*

Down the years, many theologians and biblical scholars have interpreted the salvation of the woman in the light of the doctrine of justification, understanding the impurity and sterility of the woman as an image of human sin that, according to the Law, leads to death. They have then gone on to explain the action of the woman as an act of faith, and to see Jesus' healing of her as an image of the new life offered to us in Jesus Christ, crucified and risen. As Paul describes,

> For "no human being will be justified in his sight" by deeds prescribed by the law, for through the law comes the knowledge of sin. But now, apart from law, the righteousness of God has been disclosed, and is attested by the law and the prophets, the righteousness of God through faith in Jesus Christ for all who believe. For there is no distinction, since all have sinned and fall short of the glory of God; they are now justified by his grace as a gift, through the redemption that is in Christ Jesus (Rom. 3:20b–24).

Understood in the cultural context of this Gospel story, however, Jesus' words invite us also to interpret the salvation of the woman in a wider and richer way. If we were to ask ourselves what exactly this woman is saved *from*, we might first say that she is saved from her sickness: she is made well, physically healed, as many translations explain. God is not only interested in our spiritual life, but in our physicality, in our very flesh and blood. This is made abundantly clear at the opening of John's Gospel where the author asserts, "The Word was made *flesh*" (John 1:14). It is this God *with us* whom we see in Jesus throughout the Gospels, showing compassion to the suffering and healing those who are sick. Jesus is as interested in the eyes, ears, tongue, limbs and skin of those he heals as he is in their relationship with God.

> So his fame spread throughout all Syria, and they brought to him all the sick, those who were afflicted with various diseases and pains, demoniacs, epileptics, and paralytics, and he cured them (Matt. 4:24).

But the salvation of the woman through physical healing has wider implications. Once healed of her flow of blood, she is also healed from her isolation from the community. From now on, she can live with and for others. She can re-establish normal relationships. She can be a witness to the presence of the Kingdom of the God who is not only interested in the soul, but in the whole person.

In healing the woman physically, Jesus transforms her whole life. Yet she is not the only one to be transformed. The life of the community is transformed too, enriched once again after twelve years, by her presence, her participation and her personality. The Kingdom of God is interested not only in each one, but in the community as a whole, in the depth and breadth of its life that cries out to be saved from harmful divisions, fears and hatreds.

In the local church in Wales, these reflections became increasingly important for us as our ministry amongst homeless people progressed. When Christians from other churches heard about the work we were doing, the first question they always asked me was about the number of homeless people who had started coming to church or who had had a conversion experience. I always answered as honestly as I could: most of the clients whom we welcomed did not stay for long in the area. Very often, the accommodation that was found for them by the local authority was a long way from the town and it was not surprising that we did not see them frequently again. However, several of our clients did come to services, and the conversation around the dinner table on a Sunday night in the shelter focused on the passage that we had read in the evening service. One young man had been received into membership.

Questions were rarely asked by Christians visiting us about the number of people who had been kept from having to sleep on the street in the snow or rain, or who had since moved on to proper accommodation or found employment. Few wanted to know the number of clients who had not re-offended or returned to prison. Fewer still wanted to know how many had come to feel they belonged. It was as if the Church of Jesus Christ had no place in being interested in the practical aspects of people's lives. Yet God is profoundly interested. Those who are called to "Strive first for the Kingdom of God" (Matt. 6:33) are invited to live the promise, envisioning the Kingdom that has the power to transform society.

Just as the community to which the woman returned must have been changed and enriched, so also was the community of our local church. Slowly and gradually the volunteers came to know the young people hidden behind our fears and prejudices. They came to know their stories and some of the horrendous experiences they had lived through. They came to see and understand the human beings who were just like us: people with a mixture of fear and joy in their hearts, longing for love, each and every one created in the image of God. I particularly remember one beautiful day when one of the volunteers, a young father in his thirties, with a gentle open kindness about him to melt any heart, said to me, "Any o' them could be my cousin, see."

> **Slowly and gradually the volunteers came to know the young people hidden behind our fears and prejudices.**

One Sunday during the evening service, we were sitting quietly in prayer when one of our clients who was sitting at the back of the church suddenly called out, "I can't stop burping, sorry, and I'm disturbing you, see, so I'm on my way. Seeya." From where I was standing at the front, I saw him get up to leave. I gave him a big smile and nodded, not wanting to break the quiet in the church. But at the very same moment, without my saying a word, everyone else in the church looked up, turned around as one and crooned, "Bye!", and waved. It was a wonderfully heart-warming moment.

Eighteen months earlier, some members of our church had been very wary of welcoming homeless people. They had been worried that our services might be interrupted by people who had drunk too much. They were dead right. But on this night, I could not help but smile. We had changed so much. When we had ventured out hoping to serve others in a new way, we had prayed that God would use us as agents of the Kingdom, changing lives in the town where God had placed us. We had wanted to be bringers of Good News to others in the name of Christ. But when all was said and done, we had to recognise that we, too, were the ones who had been changed. We had grown to be more welcoming, more flexible, less rigid and less fearful. The Kingdom of God had been at work in us as much as in anyone, challenging us, transforming us and reaching down, like the yeast in the whole dough, right to the bottom of our hearts.

As I reflected on all that had happened, it seemed to me that as a church we needed the people we served as much as they needed us. Each one of them had helped us to see more deeply into the mystery of the eternal love of God whose Kingdom extends to the very least of us, including to those who are isolated, or whose lives are chaotic and challenging to others. As we welcomed homeless people, we had begun to see the world through their eyes, and through the eyes of other excluded and often invisible people of our world. We had started to be aware of the way in which fears and prejudices can often be expressed as reasonable norms by the strongest voices in society. We had come painfully to realise some of the injustices caused by an over-stretched benefit system.

Above all, God had shaken us out of our comfort-zone and out of our safe Christian cocoon. He had saved us from our all too easy ways of living our faith. He had invited us to look afresh at our Scriptures and read them in the light of our experiences. We had started to see the realities of life around us reflected in them, and come to hear more readily how the Word of God addresses us with authority and wisdom. We had come to see that the yeast of the Kingdom of God cannot stay inactive on the shelf if its power is to be made known, but must be mixed into the dough of the whole human community.

Courage from God

If we cast our attention once more to our Bible story and imagine the scene, we can hear Jesus calling the woman, "my daughter". As she has dared to hope, this woman moves from exclusion to inclusion and from invisibility into a true identity. Her relationship with Jesus changes everything. It gives this woman's life a new direction. In first century society, children were under the authority of their father. When Jesus utters the words "my daughter", he places the woman under *his* authority and from this moment she is called to live according to the values of the Kingdom. Inviting this woman to have "Courage", Jesus 'en-courages' her for the way she has acted in faith and suggests that there will be opportunities to live such a faith in the future.

Dorcas Price

As a local church in Wales, we also needed this kind of "courage" if we were to be faithful to Kingdom values. Amongst the volunteers, there was Dorcas, a widow from a nearby church. She was one of a number of older people who offered time and energy to keep the project on the road, and whose help was utterly invaluable. Staff from the association with which we worked often whispered to me that they thought that older people might lack the necessary skills for dealing with our often-difficult clients, but this woman, together with all the others in the team, proved them wholly mistaken. At the beginning, she had come rather cautiously, not sure that she had the necessary gifts for the task. But she need not have worried. She had a heart of gold, a smile to win over the most awkward customer, and very quickly created good relationships with the young people who came. "She's just like my nan," one of our clients confided to me.

Since the project had started, we had been looking for an available building in the centre of the town that might be suitable for use as a permanent full-time facility that could be open all day. Twice we had made proposals to the local council but had been turned down on the grounds of their proximity to other establishments. However, we persevered until one day, the council invited us to be present at a meeting at which the subject would be discussed again, in relation to a third proposed building. We were delighted when Dorcas agreed to be there and speak.

The day of the meeting arrived. Dorcas stood before the council and recounted some of the stories of the young people with whom she had built up relationships. She knew the stories by heart. Like the yeast in the dough, the Kingdom of God had been at work within her, and she spoke with fearless understanding and commitment. Too old to be an ambassador for the Kingdom of God? Too old to be changed by Christ? Not one jot!

At the end of her speech, the mayor invited contributions from the floor. One member of the council, a middle-aged man dressed in a smart suit, got to his feet. He began, "It would have been so good if there had been a proper facility back in the days when I was homeless." There was a stunned silence. All eyes in the room were immediately glued to him. He continued to tell his story: the break-up of his marriage, how he had had to sleep in his car and how he had lost everything when he was made redundant. Something of the passion and compassion with which Dorcas had spoken had given him the courage to speak. When he sat down, there was a long pause. Then the mayor took the decision to pass to the vote. Alleluia! This time the proposal was accepted.

Some months later, a permanent centre was opened in one of the main streets in the town. Several of the volunteers who had been involved with the project in the church offered their services to the new project as members of its council or as accompaniers of its residents. The Kingdom of God, like the yeast mixed in to the dough, had been at work even in the council chamber and would continue to be active in the heart of the community. For a while, there were no more toothbrushes or socks to be seen on the shelves or the radiators of the church hall. However, a little more than a year later, a Christian association working with young people grappling drug addiction approached the church. It was looking to set up a project in our town and asked the church if it could use its premises. No problem! At the time of writing, the project is going from strength to strength.

This magnificent passage has enabled us to encounter another of the extraordinary women in Matthew's Gospel and has deepened our understanding of the welcoming, inclusive nature of the Kingdom of God. The woman with the flow of blood follows the same pattern as we have seen in the previous chapters, *pointing forward* to the life of the Kingdom. She is a victim of the divisions that society does not notice or question, but she has the faith to see far beyond them. Daring to do what no one else in need of healing has done, this courageous woman takes the initiative and actually touches Jesus herself. The strength of her belief enables her to be gloriously and adventurously subversive of the patterns of faith others in the Gospel story follow.

Matthew's story of the woman invites us to ask what isolation and exclusion our own society finds difficult to acknowledge, while the parable challenges our desire to spend our lives in a Christian bubble, surrounded by friends from our churches, and cut off from our non-church friends and neighbours. If only we were to let the imagery of the parable challenge our faith, we might find ourselves 'mixed in' for the Kingdom in some of the most hidden, unexpected and exciting places, and discovering how God heals and transforms community.

The Kingdom of heaven is this:
God's personal love for each of us, in Christ,
and that same love shared by each and every one, with each and every one.
Madeleine Delbrêl[22]

---

22 (1904–1964), French social worker and activist, writer, poet and founder of lay communities.
Pitaud, *Prier 15 Jours avec Madeleine Delbrêl*, 50.

5
Staying True: The Enduring Kingdom

~~~

I will cling to the rope God has thrown me in Jesus Christ, even when my numb hands can no longer feel it.
Sophie Scholl[23]

I always told him, "I'm going to hold steady on to you, and you've got to see me through."
Harriet Tubman[24]

For a number of years, some French friends of mine rented out one of their bedrooms to a young man apprenticed to a local *boulangerie*. Every morning, he left for work at three o'clock. He needed the time before the shop opened at seven to prepare the dough, allow it to prove, rework it and leave it again, before dividing the batch up and putting it all in the oven.

Making bread is not a process that can be hurried. The yeast is alive and needs time to accomplish its work. Jokingly, I suggested to the young man that cakes were quicker to make, and that had he chosen to become a *patissier*, he might have been able to stay in bed a little longer in the morning and leave

---

[23] (1921–43), German university student, anti-Nazi campaigner, member of the White Rose non-violent resistance group.
[24] (1820?–1913), African-American escaped slave, abolitionist, conductor on the underground railroad.

for work at a more reasonable hour. I shall never forget his passionate response. "I love making bread," he insisted, "and I wouldn't change my vocation for anything in the world. I love the rhythm of it all. I love the wonder of knowing that the yeast is still at work even when I have put the dough aside. It's a miracle! It can't be rushed and it teaches me patience."

Yeast cannot be rushed. Depending on the temperature of the atmosphere, the length of time required for the process can vary, but it is never a quick fix. I often remember the words of this young apprentice when I read the parable. The Kingdom of God is like the yeast: it takes its time. The God of eternity is faithful and loves us with infinite love. He never abandons us. Behind our weaknesses, he sees our potential and forgives us our shortcomings. Despite our slowness to react to him, he continues to work within us.

We who are in Christ, and who are called to live and work for the Kingdom of God, are invited to be patient, faithful and persevering. The one in whom we place our trust is the one who first loved us and whose goodness endures for ever.

> *For the Lord is good;*
> *his steadfast love endures forever,*
> *and his faithfulness to all generations (Ps. 100:5).*
>
> *if we are faithless, he remains faithful—*
> *for he cannot deny himself (2 Tim. 2:13).*
>
> *Let us hold fast to the confession of our hope without wavering, for he who has promised is faithful (Heb. 10:23).*

The Canaanite Woman (Matt. 15:21–28)

This is a strange, intriguing story. Perhaps it often gets hidden away in many of our churches because it presents us with so many uncomfortable corners and puzzling statements. It is easier to shy away rather than grapple with it. At first sight, it offers a picture of Jesus that is at the very least hard to interpret, not to say rather troubling or out of character. If we stay with it, however, and persevere—like the yeast—the reading reveals great depths. I confess that over the years I have become increasingly encouraged by the portrait Matthew presents of this strong, passionate and determined woman, and I believe that for those of us who seek ways to face the struggles that confront us, it is time for this woman to come into her own.

> *Jesus left that place and went away to the district of Tyre and Sidon. Just then a Canaanite woman from that region came out and started shouting, "Have mercy on me, Lord, Son of David; my daughter is tormented by a demon." But he did not answer her at all. And his disciples came and urged him, saying, "Send her away, for she keeps shouting after us." He answered, "I was sent only to the lost sheep of the house of Israel." But she came and knelt before him, saying, "Lord, help me." He answered, "It is not fair to take the children's food and throw it to the dogs." She said, "Yes, Lord, yet even the dogs eat the crumbs that fall from their masters' table." Then Jesus answered her, "Woman, great is your faith! Let it be done for you as you wish." And her daughter was healed instantly (Matt. 15:21–28).*

If we were to read this passage hurriedly, we might come up with a reading like this,

A foreign woman wanting to take advantage

of Jesus' arrival in her area asks him to heal her daughter. First of all, Jesus refuses, believing that she is outside the range of his ministry. However, the woman doggedly wears him down in order to get her own way. Jesus finally gives in to her nagging, agrees to heal the woman's daughter, and congratulates her for her faith.

However, if we were to look more closely at this story, seeking elements of the persevering Kingdom at work, we might discover many deeper insights to help us, despite all the challenges the passage represents.

The Wrong Side of the Divides

An Anonymous Woman

The woman who approaches Jesus here is a Canaanite—a Gentile. In this society, she is at a disadvantage from every possible point of view. First, she is on the wrong side of the male/female divide. We already saw in the last chapter how far relationships between men and women were governed by laws and tradition. Even women in good health could not be totally free from their association with monthly impurity. A pious Jew was expected to avoid contact with an unrelated woman in public, which is one of the reasons why the Gospel of John records the disciples' surprise when they discover Jesus in conversation with a Samaritan woman (John 4:27). When the Canaanite woman in our story approaches Jesus on her own, she is already stretching the boundaries of propriety.

A Poor Woman

Second, she is on the wrong side of the rich/poor divide. We have also already mentioned that a woman of this time was usually represented in public by a man to whom she was related, and so the appearance of this Gentile woman on her own suggests that she may have had no one to represent her. Without a patriarch to defend her rights, a woman at this time very often found herself in dire straits, so if this Canaanite woman was indeed a widow, she was likely to be poor as well.

A Foreign Woman ...

Thirdly, she is on the wrong side of the Jew/Gentile divide. She is a Canaanite woman, a Gentile. Such a word is charged with meaning, as a huge cultural divide separated Jews and Gentiles during Jesus' time. A pious Jew gave thanks to God to have been born 'not a Gentile, nor a slave nor a woman', while a righteous Greek also gave thanks to have been born 'not a barbarian, nor a slave, nor a woman'. The prophets of God pronounced the judgment of God upon his people for having allowed Canaanite religion to gain a foothold in Israel, and accused the religion of turning God's people away from the true path.

... From a Notorious Place

Worse still, this Canaanite woman comes from the region of Tyre and Sidon. Tyre, the capital of Phoenicia was well-known for its wealth built upon corruption, while Sidon, not far away, was frequently associated with it. Across the centuries, the prophets denounced them both. While Isaiah had pronounced the judgment of God on these corrupt places (Is. 23:1–8), Amos had proclaimed the word of the Lord against Tyre for having deported the Israelites into the hands of their enemies (Am. 1:10). Meanwhile, Ezekiel had prophesied against the Prince of Tyre who, seduced by a lust for wealth, had been turned away from justice.

> *In the abundance of your trade*
>   *you were filled with violence, and you sinned;*
> *so I cast you as a profane thing from the mountain of God,*
>   *and the guardian cherub drove you out*
>   *from among the stones of fire.*
> *Your heart was proud because of your beauty;*
>   *you corrupted your wisdom for the sake of your splendor.*
> *I cast you to the ground;*
>   *I exposed you before kings,*
>   *to feast their eyes on you.*
> *By the multitude of your iniquities,*
>   *in the unrighteousness of your trade,*
>   *you profaned your sanctuaries.*
> *So I brought out fire from within you;*
>   *it consumed you,*
> *and I turned you to ashes on the earth*
>   *in the sight of all who saw you (Ezek. 28:16–18).*

So, this Canaanite woman is far from having a positive cultural profile. Whether she likes it or not, the reputation of Tyre and Sidon goes before her. In the first century, individuals were thought—much more than they are today—to belong to, and represent, the family or group they came from. It is hardly surprising that the disciples of Jesus are highly suspicious of her and want Jesus to send her away. They speak of her almost as if, like her tormented daughter, she has quite taken leave of her senses, "Send her away, for she keeps shouting after us" (Matt. 15:23).

A Persevering Woman

Bearing the burden of her people's history and reputation, she could not find herself in a worse position for approaching Jesus and his disciples and asking for his help. She could well adopt a victim mentality and tell herself that her chances of being heard are so slim that there is no point trying. However, this most extraordinary woman will not allow herself to be discouraged. No matter how poor she might be socially and materially, she is rich in hope. Every time I read this story, I am amazed at the qualities of persistence and perseverance she shows in what is an urgent, delicate and extremely stressful situation.

The Testimony of Sojourner Truth

For me, one of the most powerful testimonies of Kingdom courage and perseverance comes from the nineteenth century and is offered by Sojourner Truth (1797?–1883),[25] the African-American preacher and evangelist who campaigned for the abolition of slavery. Like the Canaanite woman, she, too, stood on the wrong side of every cultural divide of her day. A black woman, she was born into slavery in Swartekill, Ulster County, in the State of New York. Named Isabelle at birth, she was known simply as Belle during her days of slavery.

Amongst the horrific injustices that led many slaves to describe their condition as nothing short of hell, slavery brought with it a broken family and a broken childhood. She was the ninth child born to her parents, but tragically never knew her brothers and sisters during her childhood. They had all been sold to other masters, as was the common practice of slaveholders. Children born to slaves were counted as the master's property and frequently sold for financial gain without any thought for the family lives that were being destroyed thereby. Belle's mother never ceased to weep

---
25 The birth dates of slaves were not recorded by masters.

for her small son and daughter who had been taken from her one day in December. They had rushed out from the basement where they lived, drawn by the sound of sleigh-bells. However, it was a fearsome trap. No sooner were the children outside than they were seized, pushed inside a box and driven away on the sleigh. Hearing her children's piercing screams, Belle's mother could only watch the sleigh disappear into the distance and never saw her children again.

As a slave, Belle received no education and remained illiterate until the end of her days. Worse still, she never learnt English as a first language. She had grown up speaking Dutch. Her first master's family were of Dutch origin, and even when, later, Belle had finally mastered English, she continued to speak it with a Dutch accent. (The master had considered it a shrewd strategy to ensure that slaves of his spoke only Dutch, as it made communication with others outside of his lands more difficult and escape virtually impossible.) When she was sold to another master who was English-speaking, she was unable to understand what she was being told to do. She was brutally beaten by her mistress, who interpreted her lack of response as disobedience.

The young Belle had, without question, every possible eventuality stacked against her: she was female, black, a slave, poor, illiterate and uneducated and unable to speak English without a strange accent. Furthermore, at a height of nearly six foot, she was powerfully and heavily built. She would even be accused in public of being a man in disguise. Yet despite so many disadvantages, she was to stand as a powerful, passionate and courageous witness to the values of the Kingdom of God.

The Foundations of Perseverance

Perseverance Founded on Love

Let us return for a moment to the Canaanite woman. What were the motivations lying behind her action? What sustained her capacity to persevere? Without doubt, she was first of all motivated by a mother's love. It is clear from her desperate tone that the Canaanite woman, rather like the synagogue official who comes to ask Jesus to heal his daughter (Matt. 9:18), is driven by love for her child. She hardly needs to spell it out in detail. Her agitated manner, her insistence, her raised voice all speak of her fear of losing her daughter. She does everything in her power to ensure that her child is brought back from death to life.

> **Sojourner Truth (cont'd)**
>
> Belle also was fundamentally motivated by love—for her own five children and for the children of others like her—and by the ways in which she had experienced suffering as a result of it. As a young woman, Belle fell in love with a slave who belonged to the master of a neighbouring property. The young man's master, however, was forcing him to marry one of his own women slaves, in the knowledge that any children born to them would also be counted as his property. Just before the marriage, the young man escaped from the property in order to be united with Belle. Unfortunately, he was found and recaptured and beaten to the point of death. Belle never saw him again. Meanwhile, Belle was forced by her own master to marry one of his slaves. He was an older man, good and honest, but Belle did not love him. They had

five children together, but later, when they had both been liberated from slavery, they parted. Neither had ever desired the union.

Belle always bore the scars of these terrifying and tragic experiences. Throughout her ministry, she carried the memory of the abuses meted out on her by an obscenely unjust system whereby one people was forced into submission by and to another. Not only as a child had she witnessed the unquenchable grief of her own mother, but, years later as an adult and a parent herself, she had had her own experience of having a child sold away. Her memory of love and loss always lay in some way behind the passion with which she campaigned against the sin of slavery. She longed to see her own children, and the children of all her people, freed from their bondage.

Perseverance Founded on Faith

The perseverance of the two women is also motivated by their faith. First, let us look at the faith of the Canaanite woman. It is striking that in approaching Jesus, this woman's words and actions become increasingly expressive of devotion. As far as her speech is concerned, she uses the language of prayer, addressing Jesus three times as "Lord". While this word was used to designate a person in authority, this title represents very much more in the context of the Gospel. This is not only the title that the disciples use when speaking to their Lord and master, but it will also become the title by which the Church will recognise its Saviour, crucified and risen. Addressing Jesus in this way, the Canaanite woman affirms Jesus' authority over her, and aligns herself with those called to be disciples.

But the expression of her faith is deeper than the use of a title. "Lord, Son of David," she shouts the first time, "Have mercy on me." This is the language of prayer and worship. We have read such phrases in the psalms.

> *Have mercy on me, O God,*
> *according to your steadfast love;* (Ps. 51:1).
>
> *But you, O Lord, are a God merciful and gracious,*
> *slow to anger and abounding in steadfast love and*
> *faithfulness.*
> *Turn to me and be gracious to me;*
> (Ps. 86:15–16a).

In echoing the ancient and traditional language of prayer, the Canaanite woman also paves the way for the future, pointing forward by her words to the language of the universal Church. Each time we say "Lord, have mercy upon us", we utter the words spoken by the Canaanite woman in Matthew's Gospel. Through her devotion and passion, she anticipates the presence of Gentiles into the Church.

The second time the woman addresses Jesus, her words are even more charged with intensity. "Lord, help me" (Matt. 15:25), she cries. Again, her words echo the language of the psalms, "The Lord is on my side to help me" (Ps. 118.7).

Yet again, her words promise the acceptance of Gentiles into the Church. The Acts of the Apostles tell how the apostle Paul, unable to enter Bithynia, goes down to Troas in Asia Minor,

> *During the night Paul had a vision: there stood a man*
> *of Macedonia pleading with him and saying, "Come*
> *over to Macedonia and help us"* (Acts 16:9).

Unbeknownst to her, this woman is forging a pathway towards the future. She reminds us that we may never know what might become of our perseverance and faith when we place them into the hands of God.

This Canaanite is not just a woman of words, however. Her faith is also expressed in her action. At the beginning of the story we read, "Just then a Canaanite woman from that region came out" (Matt. 15:22).

She takes her courage in both hands and emerges out of invisibility. She dares to be seen. Instead of staying with her daughter at home, she takes action for change. In a society in which women were not generally seen alone in public, she decides to defy custom and step into the wide world. That is not all: she dares to seek out the help of Jesus, and she, a Canaanite! What is more, our story suggests that having met this first challenge, the woman then runs after Jesus. When it seems that the disciples try to move away from her, they declare, "she keeps shouting after us" (Matt. 15:23).

Matthew points to a significant contrast between the disciples who simply approach Jesus, and the woman who energetically pursues him by shouting. However, the description of the woman's movement does not stop there, because a couple of verses later we discover that, "... she came and knelt before him" (Matt. 15:25).

As the encounter develops, both the words and the actions of this woman speak of a growing closeness to Jesus and a deepening relationship. She comes nearer and nearer to him, and finally prostrates herself before him.

It is very easy at times when we find ourselves blocked or struggling against rigid traditions to end up getting angry and express our frustration through anger and raised voices. We can hope that by shouting a little louder, others might be more inclined to listen to our point of view or change their minds. Yet this extraordinary woman shows us something rather different. Despite her agitated shouting at the beginning, she draws increasingly on the language of prayer rather than on the vocabulary of anger.

Sojourner Truth (cont'd)

Not unlike the Canaanite woman, Belle's perseverance was also underpinned by a faith that grew steadily deeper as her life went on. As a young girl, Belle had been brought up to believe in God and to say her prayers. In her autobiography—dictated, due to her illiteracy, to Olive Gilbert—Sojourner describes how her mother taught her to say the Lord's Prayer and often reminded her that God "hears and sees you".[26] Anticipating, no doubt, that one day Belle would be sold to another owner and taken from her, her mother would repeat to her, "when you are beaten, or cruelly treated, or fall into any trouble, you must ask help of him, and he will always hear and help you."[27] This was the beginning of a continual conversation with God that was to last all her life. Her mother was right to think that her daughter would one day need the strength that comes from prayer. When Belle was brutally beaten or mistreated, she would find refuge on an island in the middle of the nearby stream. There alone and hidden from view, she would weep and speak with God. She recalls that sometimes she would need to take refuge there several times a day.[28]

Belle's faith grew stronger in her adult life, thanks firstly to the witness of the couple who were instrumental

---

26 Olive Gilbert, *The Narrative of Sojourner Truth* (Charleston, SC: Booksurge Classics, 2009), p. 7.
27 Ibid.
28 Gilbert, *The Narrative of Sojourner Truth*, 37.

in obtaining her freedom. The day had been a long time coming. For some years, Belle, who had unusual strength and stature for a woman, had often been put to work on the land. One day she had been approached by a stranger who had simply said to her that if ever she needed help, she could come to his house—and he told her where to come. Years later, she still remembered this moment.

And one day, when life seemed particularly unbearable, she found the courage to escape her master's land with her baby under her arm. This in itself was already a huge act of faith and courage; there were plenty of slaves at the time who longed for freedom, but, too terrified of the consequences of being caught, never dared risk escape.

She made her way towards the stranger's house. The man in question was now too old and frail to come to her aid, but indicated another home where she would be helped. This was the home of the Wageners. The Wageners were a devout Quaker couple, passionate abolitionists, and the day that Belle stood at their door asking for help, they welcomed her with open arms. The couple were well-known in the area for their anti-slavery views, and it was not long before Belle's master was knocking on their door. As Belle was his property by law, the Wageners could not refuse to give Belle up. But they *could* offer to purchase her from him. They made him an offer that he could not refuse. When he finally left their house with money in his pocket and without his slave, the Wageners announced to Belle that she was now a free woman.

A slave no longer! Delivered out of bondage, Belle agreed to stay working for the Wageners. During the time she spent with them, her faith grew. The couple invited Belle to join them every night as they sat to pray and study the Scriptures. As she was unable to read, Belle would listen attentively. Thanks to the time she spent with the Wageners, it was often said of her, later in her life, that she knew the Bible off by heart. Her knowledge of the Scriptures not only offered one of the foundations upon which her future preaching ministry would be built, but continued throughout her life to inspire her Christian faith, her preaching and her activism as an abolitionist.

The biggest turning point in her life, however, occurred some years later. Belle was still living with the Wageners. They led a very quiet life and Belle started to miss all the friends she had known in her days of slavery. One day in a moment of weakness she "looked back into Egypt,"[29] and had a sudden desire to leave her life of quiet and uneventful freedom in order to return to her former life and friendships. However, God in his faithfulness used this moment to draw her more closely to him. Belle was on the brink of leaving the Wageners' house when she was prevented from doing so by an extraordinary and powerful experience of the presence of God. She described it later as a moment in which God was revealed to her as a bolt of lightning. According to her autobiography, the presence of God seemed to pin her to the spot. Not unlike the psalmist who asks, "Whither shall I go from thy presence?" she could not escape this strong, magnetic presence, no matter how hard she might have liked to. She would write later,

> she would now fain have hid herself in the bowels of the earth, to have escaped his dread presence.

---
29   Gilbert, *The Narrative of Sojourner Truth*, 39.

But she plainly saw that there was no place, not even in hell, where he was not; and where could she flee?[30]

There was nowhere she could flee to. Aware of the presence of evil in her life, she knew she needed someone to intercede for her before God. Her autobiography describes movingly how she had a vision of One "beaming with the beauty of holiness, and radiant with love"[31] standing sheltering her, like a friend sheltering her from the rays of a hot sun with an umbrella.

This was the point at which faith came to the fore in Belle's life and nothing would be the same again. As a girl, she had often cried out to God, begging him to destroy all whites and their descendants, such was the traumatic and unforgettable horror of the violence and abuse she experienced at their hands. Following this powerful experience of God, however, she was dramatically transformed, and later confessed that it was Jesus and not man who had 'civilised' her. Such was her experience of the love of Christ for her, Belle was given the grace to love those she had once thought of as her deadliest enemies. She wholeheartedly affirmed that from that moment on, she found it possible to love everyone, even whites, and it was this ability to love that would underpin her ministry as a speaker to white audiences. Such was her love for them that she dreaded for them the judgment that awaited those who did not repent of their slave-owning ways. She wanted to convince them of the sin of practising it.

Belle finally moved to New York City. There she

---

30 Gilbert, *The Narrative of Sojourner Truth*, 40.
31 Ibid., 41.

found work but encountered many setbacks. She had thought to save up enough money to buy a home, but she failed miserably. She hoped at one stage to exercise a ministry amongst black Christians, but her preaching was rejected. Worse still, she nearly lost her untarnished reputation when she joined a Christian community that turned out to have been founded by a charlatan who was finally accused of murder and adultery. Thanks to the intervention of friends who knew her well, her good name remained intact, but it was a close shave.

Other trials also awaited her. Just like her own mother, Belle had also known the horror of losing a child. While she had been with the Wageners, her young son Peter had been sold to another master. Thanks to the couple's encouragement, Belle had taken the master to court for the act, which was illegal at the time, of selling Peter to a slave-owner outside of the State. To the surprise of all, Belle was one of the first black women ever to win a case in court against a white man. Following this, Belle was reunited with Peter, who had been badly traumatised and abused by his experience. Despite her best efforts, Peter started to go off the rails as he grew older and Belle eventually had to experience the particular heartache of the mother whose child is sentenced to prison.

However, in spite of her failures, struggles and disappointments, God remained faithful to her. Belle began to discern a call from God to exercise a ministry as an itinerant evangelist. At the time, female preachers were generally few and far between, but there was a small number in the north-east. During a time of prayer, Belle heard God saying to her "Go east". She was about to doubt the veracity of this call when she heard the voice of God again. At that moment, she offered herself into God's service, committing herself to following his leading.

Up until this moment, Belle had always been known by the name her parents had given her at birth. She did not bear her own surname, as a slave had to be known by the name of the slave-owner. As her name 'Isabelle' would always remind her of her slavery, she decided to seek another name that would express her new identity as a free woman and as a servant of the truth. In prayer, she was given the names 'Sojourner Truth'. Many years later she explained to the author Harriet Beecher Stowe, an author and fellow-abolitionist, how her name had changed,

> When I left the house of bondage, I left everything behind. I wasn't going to keep anything from Egypt on me, so I went to the Lord and asked Him to give me a new name. The Lord gave me the name Sojourner, because I was to travel up and down the land, showing people their sins, and being a sign unto them. Afterwards I told the Lord I wanted another name, because everybody else had two names; and the Lord gave me Truth, because I was to declare the truth to the people.[32]

Conscious of God's great faithfulness to her, Sojourner was faithful to God's call on her life. The testimony of this extraordinary woman reminds us that despite our failings, God does not abandon us. None of us knows exactly where God will lead. However, we follow in the

---

[32] W. Terry Whalin, *Sojourner Truth: American Abolitionist* (Uhrichsville, OH: Barbour, 1997), p. 90.

knowledge that we can place our trust in him. When we respond to Christ's call to be disciples, we offer ourselves to him not just for a week or so, but for a whole lifetime. It is a commitment for always, in response to the God who is eternally faithful to us.

The ministry to which Sojourner was called—a ministry amongst white people—was to demand huge courage and perseverance. The evangelist was acutely aware of her need to depend on God. Sustained by her love and knowledge of Scripture, upheld by the Holy Spirit, taking strength from her experiences of the presence of God and convinced of God's call on her life, Sojourner sustained a passion for the Gospel and a message of truth and justice for decades to come. She denounced slavery in all its forms as a sin. Black and white people alike were called as brothers and sisters to work for a world in which slavery had no place.

Perseverance Sustained by Hope and a Vision of the Kingdom

The perseverance both of the Canaanite woman and of Sojourner Truth is sustained not only by motherly love, not only by a deepening relationship with Jesus, but also by hope and a passionate commitment to the values of the Kingdom of God. For the Canaanite woman, the scope of Jesus' mission and the extent of the Kingdom reach out to each and every one. This includes even her tormented daughter, who represents all that is weakest in society. In the first place, in a patriarchal society, children had no legal rights, and a girl was considered of less value than a boy. If the Canaanite woman is a widow, then her daughter is fatherless, and given that it is the mother who approaches Jesus on behalf of her daughter, we can probably assume that the daughter is unmarried. Given her current condition, she is unlikely ever to be so.

The Canaanite woman is quite extraordinary. She passionately believes that the Kingdom of God extends not only to herself, a Gentile, but even further than that: to her daughter, who is amongst the least, most invisible and most vulnerable of this world. The mother's intercession on behalf of her daughter thus has much wider significance than simply a personal request. Yes, of course, this woman is first and foremost interceding on behalf of her own child. But in believing that the Kingdom of God extends to the very poorest people of this world, she becomes a passionate intercessor for all Gentiles, and for the children of all the poorest inhabitants of the earth.

In the previous story, we discussed how different the story of the woman with a flow of blood is from other healing stories in the Gospels. The story of the Canaanite woman is also very different in character, but for different reasons. Whereas Matthew reports nothing that the woman with haemorrhages said to Jesus, in this story, the woman in question simply will not keep quiet. Far from conforming to the ideal picture of the modest, submissive woman that would have been prevalent at the time, she throws it out of the window! I am always encouraged when I reflect on the repartee that takes place between Jesus and the woman, and on the kind of daring, courageous, faith-driven persistence she shows in the face of initial rebuttal.

The Qualities of Perseverance

Unsilenced
The Canaanite Woman

Just then a Canaanite woman from that region came out and started shouting, "Have mercy on me, Lord, Son of David; my daughter is tormented by a demon." But he did not answer her at all. And his disciples came and urged him, saying, "Send her away, for she keeps shouting after us" (Matt. 15:22–23).

In this first exchange, the Canaanite woman takes the initiative and her first words are words of faith. When she calls Jesus "Son of David", she suggests that she herself is acutely aware of her own Gentile identity and that she belongs to the *others*. Yet she believes that the Kingdom extends even to Tyre and Sidon, however bad its reputation might be. It is both a monumental step of faith and a step out of line on her part. If she hopes that the scope of Jesus' ministry will extend to the likes of her, she is already living out that hope by daring—she, a Gentile—to approach Jesus, this Jewish man of authority, the Son of David. She has crossed a boundary.

I often think that this part of the story offers us a glimpse of Jesus' humanity. Mysteriously, Jesus offers no response. Why is this? Perhaps he is displaying a typical attitude of a Jew towards an unrelated woman, or towards a Gentile woman, keeping his distance. Or perhaps it is because he hesitates to exercise a ministry on disputed, Gentile soil. From the woman's point of view, however, Jesus behaves as though he has not even heard her.

However, the woman's reaction to this is not to go away downcast and disappointed, but to continue to speak. Far from conforming to the view, prevalent at the time, that a woman had to be silent in order to be thought virtuous, she perseveres. Already, we get the idea that this woman's faith is out of ordinary. This next time, in place of a silent response from Jesus and his disciples alike, she hears words that, at the very least, acknowledge her existence—this has got to be progress! However, the words are spoken not by Jesus but by the disciples who direct their comments to their Master and not her. The door has opened just a chink ... but has been closed just as swiftly.

Sojourner Truth (cont'd)

Sojourner Truth too, like the Canaanite woman, also affirmed the wide scope of the Kingdom, daring to make its values known already by crossing the boundaries and preaching to white audiences. She also found herself frequently not listened to and having to insist on being heard. From her earliest childhood, she had always loved hearing the story of the Hebrew people, especially of their deliverance from slavery in Egypt. Even though she believed that slavery had no place in the purposes of God, it was not a view held by all Christians at the time. Far from it. Many white Christians strenuously opposed her views, and not just those who were slave-owners. Those in favour of slavery argued that God had ordained slavery and created black people to be slaves. Since there were passages of the Bible that accepted the institution of slavery without question, then it could not, in their view, be counter to the will of God.

On one occasion, a man in the crowd invited Sojourner to speak of her time as a slave. The audience listened, stunned to silence, as she recounted her experience: the abominable conditions of the cellar in which her family was forced to live, her brothers and sisters being sold to other owners, being sold herself to an English-speaking master when she could only speak Dutch, and being beaten so severely that she still bore the scars deep in her flesh. She told them how she had been forbidden to marry the man she loved and forced to marry another slave of her master's choice. She was a magnificent and fiery speaker and it all poured out.

From that moment, Sojourner began to give testimony more frequently to her own experiences of slavery. The sense of her ministry grew clearer to her. Gradually she came to see how she had always been the victim of injustice: despised for the colour of her skin and made invisible because she was a woman. Committed to striving first for the Kingdom of God and his righteousness, she came to see that she had a calling from God to speak about the ways in which she had been abused. She devoted herself to denouncing the sin of slavery before her white audiences and to an endeavour to end human suffering.

People flocked to hear her. However, unsurprisingly, she was frequently rebutted. Many of her listeners would not hear of bringing an end to slavery. Neither could they accept her desire to break the silence, which had kept the truth of slavery hidden from many up to this point. On one occasion, a lawyer stood up and claimed that blacks were nothing more than apes or baboons.[33] However, undaunted, she kept speaking, refusing to be silenced. One evening, at the end of a meeting, one of her listeners shouted,

> "Old woman, I don't care any more for your talk than I do for the bite of a flea." (S)he replied, "The Lord willing, I'll keep you scratching."[34]

Insistent
The Canaanite Woman

Let us return for a moment to the story of the Canaanite woman. She is nothing short of unique: unique in approaching

---
33 Whalin, *Sojourner Truth*, 153.
34 Robert Ellsberg, *Blessed Among All Women* (Spring Valley, NY: Crossroad Publishing, 2007), p. 154.

Jesus on Gentile soil, unique in being refused, and unique in not taking "no" for an answer. Faced with a refusal, she doubles her efforts. Here she is in action,

> *He answered, "I was sent only to the lost sheep of the house of Israel." But she came and knelt before him, saying, "Lord, help me" (Matt. 15:24–25).*

On the face of it, there seems to be no question that, at this moment in the story, Jesus is expressing his conviction that the Canaanite and her daughter do not belong within the scope of his ministry. The problem comes not so much from her Gentile *identity*, because already in the Gospel Jesus has come to the help of Gentile people on Jewish soil. Here, however, Jesus is outside of Jewish *territory* and it would seem that here he is unwilling to act. We might well be forgiven for asking why Jesus responds with such harshness. Some Biblical scholars suggest that Jesus wants to put the faith of the woman to the test. If this were to be the case, this episode would be the only one in the Gospel in which Jesus does not immediately offer his help, and we might ask why in this particular case he seems to be lacking in compassion.

Other scholars suggest that this story recounts the moment when Jesus' own thinking about his mission undergoes development. Here at the beginning of the dialogue, Jesus expresses his belief that God has sent him principally to the house of Israel, but by the end of the dialogue, his position has become more nuanced. Does he change in the course of the encounter?

The view that Jesus was called to develop spiritually in the course of his ministry can seem troublesome, and sits uncomfortably with the picture of the One who knows all things. However, we usually have no difficulty understanding Jesus' physical development: we accept that Jesus, who was fully human, was born a baby and had to learn to walk and talk, and grew through childhood, and adolescence to manhood. Similarly, we have no difficulty understanding that there must have been an intellectual development: he must have learnt the trade of a carpenter at his father's side, and learnt to read the Scriptures at a certain age. And there must have been skills that he never learnt, like fishing, perhaps, or weaving.

If we can recognise that Jesus had to develop physically and intellectually, why not also accept that he had to do so spiritually? In what sense would Jesus' temptations in the desert be true temptations if he knew without question what he was going to do? And why would Jesus pray in the garden of Gethsemane, "My Father, if it is possible, let this cup pass me by" (Matt. 26:39), if he did not hold a glimmer of hope that he might escape the very suffering and death he had announced three times over?

If a spiritual evolution is possible at the time of his temptations and sufferings, why not also during his conversation with the Canaanite woman? It may be that his encounter with the Canaanite woman enables Jesus to see his earthly ministry in a wider context. Perhaps, here, he understands that, exceptionally, he can heal on Gentile soil. If this is indeed the case, his encounter with the Canaanite woman would be the first and only one in the Gospel to provide the context in which he changes his mind. This story then becomes one that points towards the authority that the risen Christ will one day have in all the world.

Or again, we might want to see this episode as the moment when Jesus takes the opportunity to teach his disciples something important. At the approach of the woman, the disciples respond in a typically Jewish way towards a Gentile woman. Their immediate reaction is to think that Jesus should have nothing to do with such a person, and that he should send her away without question. It may be that Jesus, the great teacher, wants to lead his disciples to a better understanding of the Kingdom of God. He begins the conversation by adopting a typically Jewish point of view, but then continues the conversation by demonstrating that a change in point of view is necessary. If we were to accept this interpretation, we would understand this story as a dialogue between Jesus, the Canaanite woman *and his disciples*. By means of this teaching strategy, Jesus prepares his disciples for the moment when they will be called to recognise the presence of faith in Gentile people as missionaries of the early Church.

Insightful and Visionary
The Canaanite Woman

In the ancient world, women, who were not usually given the opportunity to learn to read, were not associated with being intelligent. As a result, they were deemed to be unworthy of being listened to. This woman defies expectations. Shy, modest and retiring? Not one bit of it! Just listen to her quick-wittedness,

> *He answered, "It is not fair to take the children's food and throw it to the dogs." She said, "Yes, Lord, yet even the dogs eat the crumbs that fall from their masters' table" (Matt. 15:26–27).*

Here Jesus repeats his refusal and uses a metaphor that might well seem shocking. Here, "the children" refer to the Jews and "the dogs" refer to the Gentiles. It was a traditional way of perceiving the divide between them. As Gentiles lived outside the Law of Moses, Jews often compared them to animals living *outside* of the house. Jesus' response to the woman thus describes his fear of the poor children (the Jews) being deprived of their meal because their food has been thrown to waste outside for the dogs (the Gentiles).

If the woman is shocked by the way Jesus has spoken to her, she does not show it. She perseveres with insight and intelligence. With a combination of wit, vision and theological clarity, she responds with faith, "Yes, Lord."

But even as she appears to accept what he says, she also finds an ingenious way of presenting a different point of view. When she hears the analogy of children and dogs, she instinctively knows that Jesus is picturing the dogs being *outside of the house*. However, as he has not made this explicit, this gives her the room to reframe what he says. She intentionally assumes the dogs he refers to are *inside* the house. This allows her to agree with him ("Yes, Lord") that food should not be wasted by being thrown *outside*! But it also allows her to make her point: since the dogs are already in the house, there is no need to do that in the first place! In fact, there is a way to feed them without wasting any food at all. As the dogs sit under the table, they can simply eat the excess food that falls from the children's table.

The woman's brilliant and insightful re-reading of Jesus' words enables her to reinterpret what he says without rudely contradicting him. More importantly, it opens up a radical new paradigm. The children (the people of Israel) and the dogs (the Gentiles) are not separated by the walls of the house (some within the boundaries of Jesus' ministry, some outside them). Rather, they are all inside, belonging to the same household. The Canaanite woman has no doubt at all that there is more than enough bread, to the extent that the dogs under the table will be able to eat the leftovers.[35] A true theologian, she believes that the Kingdom of God has no divides. She has such faith in Jesus and such confidence in the abundant generosity of God that she trusts Jesus' ministry on Gentile soil will not come at a compromise to his ministry to the Jews at all.

---

35   Clements, *Mothers on the Margin?*, 223.

Sojourner Truth (cont'd)

Before we consider Jesus' response to the woman and the reasons for it, let us turn back for a moment to Sojourner Truth. This woman also passionately believed that all people, white and black, belonged to the same household, and, like the Canaanite woman, was not short of intelligent repartee to make her point. On one occasion, a young revivalist in the audience stood up. He firmly supported the continuation of slavery and had been shocked and outraged at what Sojourner had said. He found it impossible to believe that anyone who argued for the abolition of slavery could possibly be in a right relationship with God. He told her therefore that she needed to be reconciled with God. She replied,

> Reconciled with God! Why, I ain't got nothing against God! Why should I be reconciled to Him for? God's always been mighty good to me; He called me out of slavery and has taken good care of me ever since. You ministers would have kept me in bondage. Why, I haven't got anything against Him.[36]

Slowly, Sojourner began to understand that black and enslaved women had a double need to be freed from injustice: both as slaves, and as women. At the time, white women were campaigning to be accorded the same rights as white men. This powerful movement was slow to recognise the situation of black women who, once liberated from slavery, still did not have the same rights as black men freed from slavery. As Sojourner said,

---

36   Whalin, *Sojourner Truth*, 119.

If colored men get their rights, and not colored women, colored men will be masters over the women, and it will be just as bad as before.[37]

Sojourner was intent that questions regarding the rights of black women should not be forgotten. She reacted strongly when arguments presented for or against the rights of women revolved solely around the experience of white women. When she heard the view expressed that women should long for nothing more than to stay at home to bring up their children, she hastened to remind the company that she would have liked nothing better than to stay at home with her children—but that as a slave she was sent out to work in the fields.

Her improvised speech, made in 1851 at the Women's Rights Convention in Ohio, responded to those who argued that God had made women too frail to be accorded equal civil rights. Denouncing any idea of female frailty, her words are an expression of her faith, her perseverance, not to say her courage, wit and humour. She remarks,

> May I say a few words? I want to say a few words about this matter.
> I am a woman's rights.
> I have as much muscle as any man, and can do as much work as any man. I have plowed and reaped and husked and chopped and mowed, and can any man do more than that?
> I have heard much about the sexes being equal; I can carry as much as any man, and can eat as much

---

[37] Ellsberg, *Blessed Among All Women*, 154.

too, if I can get it. I am as strong as any man that is now.[38]

Sojourner was always careful not to criticise the churches that stood in support of slavery. In contrast to those abolitionists who wanted to denounce them, Sojourner refused to do so. "We ought to be like Christ," she argued. "He said, 'Father, forgive them; for they know not what they do.'"[39] Approaching her audiences with great hopefulness, she was passionately opposed to any idea of civil war. She forgave those who had mistreated her and affirmed that she would offer them food and drink if ever they appeared destitute at her door. Her vision of the Kingdom was wide. Just as the Canaanite woman's request is drawn against a political background, so the struggle in which Sojourner was engaged also had huge and complex political dimensions, fraught with ambiguities. However, she remained faithful to the God who had delivered her out of slavery. He had forgiven her and drawn her to himself. She persevered.

The perseverance of both the Canaanite woman and Sojourner Truth speaks powerfully to us of our need for a powerful vision of the Kingdom. Often we can hear testimonies in our churches that declare, "We didn't have any trouble, the doors opened. God was with us!" Or, "it all went through easily; God is on our side!" Then on the occasions when we encounter opposition, we prefer to perceive that God has closed the door on a project rather than believing that he is calling us to

---

38   From the version of the speech published in 1851 by Rev. Marius Robinson in the *Anti-Slavery Bugle*.
39   Whalin, *Sojourner Truth*, 120.

persevere. It is easy to repeat the words 'triumph' and 'victory' as though a testimony that speaks of failure and struggle has little value or validity. We can be in danger of choosing only to fight little battles or to rejoice in little victories, and of shying away from complicated struggles for fear that the victory might not be won without years of prayer and perseverance.

The world that God loves still suffers injustices and oppression of all kinds. We who are called to serve the Kingdom have an important witness to offer. New forms of slavery, including many that make prisoners of women, rear their ugly heads, alongside the racisms that are as old as the hills. There is no time to lose. The epistle to the Hebrews encourages us,

> *Therefore, since we are surrounded by so great a cloud of witnesses, let us also lay aside every weight and the sin that clings so closely, and let us run with perseverance the race that is set before us, looking to Jesus the pioneer and perfecter of our faith (Heb. 12:1–2a).*

Two Women of the Kingdom

The story of the Canaanite woman finishes in an extraordinary way, with Jesus endorsing the truth of what the woman has said,

> *Then Jesus answered her, "Woman, great is your faith! Let it be done for you as you wish." And her daughter was healed instantly (Matt. 15:28).*

Of course, we who read the story in the light of resurrection faith and in the knowledge of the Gospel are hardly surprised to find that Jesus agrees to heal the Gentile woman's daughter. Yet in terms of the cultural divides of Jesus' day, it is astonishing. Why exactly does Jesus accept what the woman says and agree to heal her child?

To begin with, Jesus has been ready to listen to this woman. Unlike his disciples who, at the beginning, were all for sending her away, Jesus has allowed her to approach. Moreover, he has taken the conversation with her seriously. Rather than glossing over her remarks or interrupting her, he has engaged with her with an openness of spirit reflective of the openness of the Kingdom.

As a result, he has come to recognise her extraordinary spiritual qualities. At the end of the story, he agrees to heal her daughter not because her remarks are clever or witty, but because by means of this brilliance, she has communicated both her faith and her far-reaching insight. Coming from a place of disadvantage and anguish, from the 'wrong' side of the divides, she believes in an enormous God whose love is not fenced in by human boundaries.

Expressing amazement, Jesus commends the woman for her faith. It is "great" not only in terms of her dogged perseverance, but also because of the magnitude of the vision she has shared. She has stayed true to her trust in the generous God, and his capacity to overcome every divide. As a result, her faith has opened a new dimension for Jesus' ministry and anticipated the Christian community of the future.

For the woman, Jesus' promise of healing for her daughter is the moment when her trust in him comes to fruition. Her vision of the "children" and "dogs" sharing "food" is confirmed. She returns home having caught sight, before time, of the promise of a new community in which Jews and Gentiles will eat together. It is not just her daughter who is healed: through her persevering faith in Jesus, she has glimpsed the healing of cultural rifts which are centuries old.

Sojourner Truth (cont'd)

Sojourner Truth also glimpsed the healing of divides. She had the joy of hearing her old master confess that he regretted his part in slavery. In 1849, she returned to see her eldest daughter, who had remained living with her old master. Of all the slave-owners she had served, this one had been the most humane, and Sojourner was thrilled to hear him denounce slavery as "the wickedest thing in the world", and "the greatest curse the earth had ever felt",

> ... In my slaveholding days, there were few who spoke against it, and these few made little impression on any one. Had it been as it is now, think you I could have held slaves? No! I should not have dared to do it, but should have emancipated every one of them.[40]

We might not be surprised to find that Sojourner's autobiography concludes on a note of forgiveness,

> Oh! how sweet to my mind was this confession! And what a confession for a master to make to a slave! A slaveholding master turned to a brother! Poor old man, may the Lord bless him, and all slave-holders partake of his spirit![41]

What faith! What hope! What love!

---

40 Gilbert, *The Narrative of Sojourner Truth*, 75.
41 Ibid.

The story of the Canaanite woman offers a wonderful portrait of persevering faith. Approaching Jesus and asking him to heal her daughter, this woman announces her belief that the Kingdom extends even to the most forgotten and invisible people of the world. Far from being quiet, reticent and retiring, she uses all her wit, understanding and intelligence in her encounter with Jesus and convinces him to heal her daughter even on Gentile soil. Instead of offering him a picture of a truly *traditional* woman, she offers him a picture of a truly *faithful* one.

Undoubtedly, the Canaanite woman understands little of the implications of her faith or her perseverance. However, she points to the day when Gentiles will be welcomed into the Church. When we allow God to give us perseverance, resilience and irrepressible determination, we never know where it will lead. The presence of the yeast, at work in our hearts, may well in time open doors of which we have not yet even dreamed.

> *Never give up, for that is just the place and the time*
> *that the tide will turn.*
> Harriet Beecher Stowe[42]

---

42   (1811–1896), American writer and abolitionist, author of *Uncle Tom's Cabin*.

6 Loving Action: The Powerful Kingdom

~~~

People must not only hear about the Kingdom of God, but must see it in actual operation, on a small scale perhaps and in imperfect form, but a real demonstration nonetheless.
Pandita Ramabai[43]

If you can't feed a hundred people, then feed just one.
Mother Teresa[44]

Far the greatest things grow by God's law out of the smallest.
Florence Nightingale[45]

The woman of our parable uses a huge quantity of flour in relation to the yeast; three measures of flour. Such an amount represented as much as the hands of a single woman could possibly knead. A great contrast lies at the heart of the parable. On the one hand, there is the smallness of the yeast, hidden and invisible, and on the other, the enormous amount of flour. We might see a similar comparison in the parable of

---

43   (1858–1922), Indian reformer. Ellsberg, *Blessed Among All Women*, 156.
44   (1910–1997), Albanian-Indian religious, school-teacher, headmistress and founder of the Missionaries of Charity.
45   (1820–1910), English nurse and medical reformer.

the mustard seed, which contrasts the tiny dimensions of the seed with the grandeur of the tree that grows from it (Matt. 13:31–32).

It seems nothing short of miraculous that a derisory quantity of yeast could possibly have such a dramatic effect. If we did not know better, we might assume that the greater weight of flour would easily annihilate the effect of the yeast, or prevent it from working at all. However, yeast has an extraordinary power, and the parable reminds us that what appears large and mighty in the eyes of the world is not necessarily what is most powerful in the Kingdom of God. On the contrary: the action that seems insignificant in the eyes of the world can have extraordinary strength when it is offered to God.

We often feel that when it comes to our witness, our efforts are only too feeble. We fall into the trap of fervent activity out of fear that smaller actions are less worthy or may lie forgotten. We are hurt when our hard-working endeavours to serve go unnoticed by the community of the local church. However, Jesus invites us to see our lives from a different perspective. When the yeast of the Kingdom is at work, the most humble and hidden actions have eternal significance.

> *He sat down opposite the treasury, and watched the crowd putting money into the treasury. Many rich people put in large sums. A poor widow came and put in two small copper coins, which are worth a penny. Then he called his disciples and said to them, "Truly I tell you, this poor widow has put in more than all those who are contributing to the treasury. For all of them have contributed out of their abundance; but she out of her poverty has put in everything she had, all she had to live on" (Mark 12:41–44).*

> "For truly I tell you, if you have faith the size of a mustard seed, you will say to this mountain, 'Move from here to there,' and it will move; and nothing will be impossible for you" (Matt. 17:20).

The Woman Who Anoints Jesus' Head (Matt. 26:6–13)

The story of the woman in Bethany who anoints Jesus' head is one that we may often hear during Holy Week, in the days leading up to Good Friday. For this reason, it is more prominent than some of the other stories of women in Matthew's Gospel. Ironically, however, it describes a rather hidden event that takes place in the home of Simon the leper, away from the gaze of both the authorities and the crowd. It is one of my favourite stories in the Scriptures. It recounts not a dramatic event or a stupendous miracle performed before crowds, but simply and tenderly describes a significant act carried out by an unnamed woman. It is a really small action, but one that magnificently reveals the faith of the woman who performs it, and speaks of the powerful Kingdom to which, prophetically, she points.

Now while Jesus was at Bethany in the house of Simon the leper, a woman came to him with an alabaster jar of very costly ointment, and she poured it on his head as he sat at the table. But when the disciples saw it, they were angry and said, "Why this waste? For this ointment could have been sold for a large sum, and the money given to the poor." But Jesus, aware of this, said to them, "Why do you trouble the woman? She has performed a good service for me. For you always have the poor with you, but you will not always have me. By pouring this ointment on my body she has prepared me for burial. Truly I tell you, wherever this good news is proclaimed in the whole world, what she has done will be told in remembrance of her." (Matt. 26:6–13).

If we were to skim over this story, we might come up with an interpretation such as this,

> A woman of ill repute comes into Simon's house and pours perfume onto Jesus' head. It is an act of welcome, but Jesus uses the moment to refer once again to his forthcoming death. At a time in history when dead bodies needed to be anointed before they were placed in a tomb, Jesus explains that the woman has prepared his body for burial. Jesus supports her act against the criticism expressed by his disciples.

However, a more careful reading of the passage, which seeks the signs of the powerful Kingdom made known in the smallest action, leads us both to a deeper understanding of the story, and to a richer appreciation of the woman's initiative.

Who is the Woman?

We know nothing of this woman, where she comes from, or what her family background is. She is anonymous. Down the centuries, the Church very often associated her with the one who appears in Luke's Gospel (Luke 7:36–50). Even if both stories are about an anointing, the details are quite different. In his Gospel, Luke writes about a woman who enters the house of a *Pharisee*—a pious Jew—to anoint the *feet* of Jesus, whereas Matthew describes how she enters the home of a *leper* and anoints Jesus' *head*. Luke's episode take place in *Galilee*, whereas Matthew's story takes place in *Bethany*, a village not far from Jerusalem. Luke's story takes place during the *general ministry* of Jesus, whereas Matthew's occurs just before the *passion* of Jesus. In Luke's story, the Pharisee considers the woman to be of doubtful moral standing. However, in

Matthew's Gospel, none of the characters that are present in the house accuse the woman of being a prostitute.

What might we deduce about this woman in Matthew's story? Instead of seeing her as a woman of the street, we might rather think of her as a woman with money at her disposal. Matthew tells us that she offers a perfume of great price. What poor woman would have such a costly substance in her possession? The comment of the disciples certainly seems to suggest that they do not count the woman to be amongst the poor, "For this ointment could have been sold for a large sum, and the money given to the poor" (Matt. 26:9).

The Power of Action

The Woman Who Anoints Jesus

This woman's act takes probably only a few minutes, nothing more. She utters no words, and offers no explanation for what she is doing. However, her act, not unlike that of Simon of Cyrene, who will carry Jesus' cross (Matt. 27:32), speaks more powerfully than any speech or sermon.

Very often when we speak of someone 'giving their testimony', we think in terms of the words that they speak. We can be in danger of thinking that what counts the most in 'testimony' is the verbal proclamation of the Gospel. We think we have to explain everything: the love of God, his forgiveness of sin offered to all through the death of Jesus on the cross, the joy of faith. However, this wonderful episode included in Matthew's Gospel speaks simply of an act, so powerful, so significant and so prophetic, that it will always be remembered. Jesus congratulates the woman for what she has done, "Truly I tell you, wherever this good news is proclaimed in the whole world, what she has done will be told in remembrance of her" (Matt. 26:13).

Amy Carmichael

The witness of the woman with the perfume, whose silent act speaks more powerfully than words, is wonderfully mirrored in the life of Amy Carmichael (1867–1951), who worked as a missionary in South India. Although she wrote numerous books,[46] she is remembered not really for her words but for the beauty of her actions.

On her arrival in South India, she worked alongside the Walkers. They were a missionary couple who had established an itinerant ministry visiting the traditional Hindu villages in the region and announcing the Gospel. Amy was to lead a team who would minister to the village women. (In certain aspects of her ministry, Amy was very much a missionary of her time. These days, many of her methods might seem to us to be lacking in cultural understanding and sensitivity.) For many months, the women in Amy's team laboured away with little result. People in the villages were sceptical, showed little interest in what the Christians had to say, and at times Amy despaired.

However, one day, a young girl from a Hindu family took the decision to break caste and follow Christ. In such a traditional environment, her decision was to have dire consequences, and she received death threats from members of her family as well as from people of the village. The missionaries were able to offer her protection away from home, and a few months later she was baptised. The repercussions of the baptism were equally devastating, this time both for the mission whose school was set on fire, and for the missionaries

---

46 For a bibliography, see Iain H. Murray, *Amy Carmichael: 'Beauty for Ashes'* (Edinburgh, UK: Banner of Truth Trust, 2015), pp. 160–161.

themselves who received warnings from the authorities.

As time went on, the evangelists began to hear of the life awaiting some young girls who, due to the poverty of their family or as a result of a family vow or tradition, were sold to Hindu temples. Following the customary practices of the system, these young girls became prostitutes, and were trained to see their profession, earning money for the priests, as service to the gods. It was a form of forced prostitution of children sometimes no older than six or seven years of age. The evangelists started to pray outside temple walls.

The itinerant ministry continued, still with little result. The words the women spoke did not seem to have the impact for which Amy longed. However, one morning, when she was drinking tea on her veranda, Amy was approached by a Christian woman who had walked from a distant village. She was holding a very small girl by the hand. The child rushed towards Amy, who put her on her lap and kissed her[47] "My name is Pearl-eyes," the little girl said, "and I want to stay here always. I have come to stay."[48]

From this moment, Amy's ministry took off in earnest. The small *act* of welcoming this child proved to be more powerful than years of itinerant evangelism. Pearl-eyes had been sold to the temple by her mother, who could no longer afford to keep her. The child had escaped a first time from the temple and had found her way home, but had immediately been taken, screaming, back to the temple. In the weeks that followed, the girl had heard other prostitutes describing Amy as 'the child-stealing ammal.' They hoped to frighten her and

---

47   Murray, *Amy Carmichael*, 31.
48   Elisabeth Elliot, *A Chance to Die: The Life and Legacy of Amy Carmichael* (Grand Rapids, MI: Revell, 1987), p. 168.

discourage her from any future attempts at a getaway. However, the child decided that Amy was just the person she wanted to find. Managing to escape a second time, Pearl-eyes wandered off, and was found in the evening by the Christian woman who had brought her to Amy. The missionary welcomed Pearl-eyes as a gift from God. For Amy, these children who were the very least in the eyes of society were the first in the Kingdom of God.

Pearl-eyes was the first of many children saved from abandonment or prostitution, or from other terrible fates. Amy welcomed them into life at the mission, all the while working at a political level to reform the laws that permitted the abuse of children in this way. Amy's act of welcome led to a ministry that was a creative and innovative departure from the usual style of work practised by Evangelical missionaries at the time, which attempted to reach the sons of the upper classes. They would set up educational establishments in the belief that through the education of those with influence, the Gospel would filter into the whole of society. Amy, however, dared to be different, stepping outside the well-tried and well-trodden path of witness. Supported by the Walkers, she focused her attention on the children of the poorest people. Hidden from sight, they lay at the bottom of the pile.

It is interesting to reflect on the relationship that existed between Amy's testimony given in words, and that which was offered by her actions. It is certainly the case that the first conversion came about principally through the verbal proclamation of the Gospel. But without the action of offering protection to the converted girl, she would never have become known as the 'child-stealer'. The beginnings of Amy's ministry were essentially built upon this first action. For a while she continued with the itinerant evangelism. However, there came a point when her work amongst children had grown so much that she no longer had time for the tours. The 'new' work became her lifetime's call.

However, there were times when Amy felt exhausted. She was tired of constantly asking for God's help every time she prayed. One evening when she was feeling particularly downcast, she had a vision in which she saw olive trees all around the house. Beneath them, a man was kneeling in prayer. She knew immediately that the Lord was interceding for the children. She felt the burden lift from her shoulders and be taken onto his. She realised that she did not need to keep asking her Lord to share her burden: he was asking her to share his. Later, she wrote in her journal, "Who could have done anything but go into the garden and kneel down beside Him under the olive trees?"[49]

Loving Action that Proclaims the Kingdom

The Woman Who Anoints Jesus

Just like Amy's welcome of Pearl-eyes, the woman's anointing of Jesus' head with perfume also speaks volumes. It is not some throwaway action, but one with profound meaning. We shall need to look at the woman's act in a little more detail, in order to better understand its significance.

First of all, the woman's act announces that Jesus is already walking the way of the Cross. Jesus says, "By pouring this ointment on my body she has prepared me for burial" (Matt. 26:12).

---
49   Elliot, *A Chance to Die*, 181.

This woman knows that Jesus is going to his death. She is not the only one, of course, to understand that Jesus must die: the enemies of Jesus have been plotting it all along! When we read this story, we do so in the knowledge of the violent backdrop against which it is told.

Often when we think of the whole sweep of the Gospel story, we associate the elements of opposition with Jesus' arrival with his disciples in Jerusalem. We think of the high priests and the elders who condemn him to death. Yet this opposition has been going on since the beginning of his ministry. A closer reading of the Gospel reveals that these same elements of opposition to the Kingdom of God are present throughout the Gospel story, not least starting with Herod's slaughter of the innocents (Matt. 2:16). This opposition grows stronger and looms larger as the Gospel story progresses.

In the first part of his Gospel, Matthew presents the Pharisees as Jesus' principal opponents. A zealous group, they begin by questioning Jesus' disciples (Matt. 9:11) before moving on to interrogate Jesus himself (Matt. 12:2). Unable to see the presence of the Kingdom in Jesus, Matthew recounts how the Pharisees see the 'king of demons' at work in him (Matt. 9:34; 12:24). As far as they are concerned, Jesus is a serious troublemaker and they want him dead. Despite their calling to be faithful to the Law, they become increasingly drawn into a mire of corruption. When Jesus heals a man with a paralysed hand we read, "But the Pharisees went out and conspired against him, how to destroy him" (Matt. 12:14).

Gradually, Scriptures reveal that the Pharisees start to create alliances with other groups in order to bring pressure to bear on Jesus. In doing so, it allows us to glimpse the murky world of deals and politicking that is constantly going on in the background. First, the Pharisees oppose Jesus in alliance with the *local* scribes (Matt. 12:38). Then, during Jesus' ministry in Galilee a little later on, the Pharisees approach Jesus together with the scribes *from Jerusalem* (Matt. 15:1). It seems that in the intervening time, the local scribes have passed on their concerns to scribes in higher places. The latter have been sufficiently alarmed by the reports that they actually travel to confront Jesus in person.

After this, it is the Sadducees' turn to appear with the Pharisees (Matt. 16:1) and finally the Herodians' (Matt. 22:15–16). Meanwhile, the scribes start to oppose Jesus in conjunction with the highest authorities: the high priests and the elders (Matt. 26:57; 59). Certainly, these diverse groups at the heart of Israel held different points of view on many issues. However, Matthew recounts how, despite their differences, they create closer and closer alliances with each other in order to build an ominous opposition to Jesus. They have this terrible interest in common.

When Jesus speaks about his death for the first time (Matt. 16:21), he predicts that he will suffer at the hands of the elders, the high priests and the scribes—an alliance between the most influential authorities. It will be these groups who will condemn him for blasphemy (Matt. 26:65) and mock him at the moment of the crucifixion (Matt. 27:41). What has happened to the Pharisees meanwhile? At the very time of Jesus' suffering, the Pharisees seem to be the only ones who are absent, without links to the high priests. However, towards the end of the Gospel, when Matthew describes events that take place the day following Jesus' death, we discover that this pernicious alliance between the Pharisees and the high priests has been in existence after all, "The next day, that is, after the day of Preparation, the chief priests and the Pharisees gathered before Pilate" (Matt. 27:62). By this small detail, Matthew suggests that all the different groups, at every level, are united in their opposition to Jesus.

If now we return to the story of the woman with the perfume, we find that at the time of her anointing Jesus, his enemies are finally poised to take action. A few verses before we read,

> *Then the chief priests and the elders of the people gathered in the palace of the high priest, who was called Caiaphas, and they conspired to arrest Jesus by stealth and kill him (Matt. 26:3–4).*

Jesus' enemies and the woman all know that Jesus is bound for death. But of course, there is a fundamental difference between them. While the enemies of Jesus plot to bring Jesus' death about, she, offering her perfume, stands on Jesus' side. She may well be putting herself in danger by associating with Jesus. In such a tense political environment, the authorities may stop at nothing to be rid of anyone they perceive to be a danger to them.

Yet this woman stands not only in a different place to the enemies of Jesus, but also offers a stark contrast to the apostles. One day, as missionaries of the early Church, these apostles will be proud to announce the death of Jesus on the cross. However, during Jesus' ministry, these same followers cannot come to terms with the prospect of Jesus' death. When Jesus announces his death for the first time, it is just Peter who refuses to accept it,

> *And Peter took him aside and began to rebuke him, saying, "God forbid it, Lord! This must never happen to you" (Matt. 16:22).*

When he predicts his death for the second time, all the disciples react, and their reaction is hardly better than Peter's was, for "they were greatly distressed" (Matt. 17:23).

The third announcement of the Passion is followed by the great debate, in which the mother of James and John approaches Jesus and asks for her sons to be accorded places of honour in the Kingdom (Matt. 20:20–28). This story, which we shall be looking at closely in the next chapter, is probably one we know well. The conversation that takes place shows clearly that the disciples have yet to take the true nature of the Kingdom on board at this point.

Meanwhile, however, in contrast to the incomprehension of the disciples, the woman in our story understands only too well what the Kingdom is about. Without uttering a single word of protest or denial, she anoints Jesus "beforehand for burial". She expresses her faith through her silent, expressive witness. In so doing, she points to the values to live by, ones that are categorically different to those that the enemies of Jesus espouse and the disciples of Jesus still cling to. Her act of anointing Jesus points to his sacrifice.

However, let us not draw a line under our exploration quite yet. The woman's act has a second significance: it points to Jesus' kingship; his Messiahship. The act of anointing Jesus' head is rich with deeper meaning and echoes the words of David,

> *You prepare a table before me*
> *in the presence of my enemies;*
> *you anoint my head with oil (Ps. 23:5).*

It is reminiscent also of the anointing of a king, such as Jehu, for example,

> *Then take the flask of oil, pour it on his head, and say,*
> *"Thus says the Lord: I anoint you king over Israel" (2*
> *Kings 9:3).*

By her act, this woman shows that she has understood the true nature of Jesus' kingship. Meanwhile, others in the

Gospel story are a very long way from accepting it. The story of Jesus' Passion is full of moments of high dramatic irony in which certain characters announce the truth with regard to Jesus, without ever remotely realising that they are doing so. Believing that they are describing a blasphemous *untruth*, Jesus' murderers in fact announce what we know to be *true* when they nail Jesus to the cross the words, "This is Jesus, the King of the Jews" (Matt. 27:37). The governor's soldiers make the same ironic mistake when they mock Jesus saying "Hail, King of the Jews" (Matt. 27:29). It is equally true for the passers-by who, thinking to mock Jesus, refer to him as the King of Israel.

The passers-by and the Jewish authorities are particularly lacking in understanding. For them, Jesus could prove his identity as King of the Jews by coming down off the cross. But of course, the truth lies in the absolute opposite of this: Jesus affirms his identity as the King of Jews precisely in not coming down from the cross. Faithful to God and to the commitments he made at the time of the temptations (Matt. 4:1–11), Jesus does not put God to the test.

In the midst of this desert of faith, the woman's act is wonderfully powerful, rich with meaning. At one level, the woman, as Jesus has said, has prepared his body for burial and affirms that he is on his way to the cross. At the same time, she proclaims that the crucified one is also the King of the Jews, the anointed One. This one, tiny act, carried out by an unknown woman, speaks volumes, announces Truth. It proclaims the greatness of the Kingdom of God.

And that is why, at the end of the episode, Jesus declares that the woman's act will be remembered for always. What the woman does is far more than an act of worship, a gesture of personal faith, or a prediction of the future. Rather, it is so charged with prophetic meaning that even when the Gospel is announced to the nations, it will lose none of its significance.

The woman's act proclaims the truth of Jesus' identity and points to the mystery of the crucified Christ that lies at the heart of the Kingdom of God.

Amy Carmichael (cont'd)

Just like the act of the woman with the perfume, Amy's actions also spoke of the values of the Kingdom. As far as Amy was concerned, all her actions, even the very smallest ones, needed to be a testimony to the Kingdom and offered to the service of the King. She always remembered an episode from her early life as a missionary that had taught her a very poignant lesson. She had begun her missionary life in Japan in an area where the climate was particularly harsh. One particularly cold day, she had been to see an old Japanese woman of insubstantial means. The old lady had invited her as she wanted to hear more of the message that Amy was bringing. Having talked long and well with the woman, Amy was on the brink of inviting her to make a commitment to Christ. But suddenly, the woman noticed the fur gloves that Amy had put on as protection against the cold. At that moment, a huge economic and cultural gulf opened up between them that interrupted the conversation. Amy described later how she rushed home, took off her English clothes and put on a Japanese kimono.[50]

From that moment, Amy was acutely aware of the importance of her actions. Actions that seemed very small and wholly insignificant to her could have great meaning to someone else. They could stand completely in the way of others receiving her Christian testimony.

---
50   Elliot, *A Chance to Die*, 73.

When Amy finally arrived in India to work, she did things differently from the way other missionaries had habitually worked. Photos taken of her during the 1920s show her entirely dressed as an Indian. Conscious of the whiteness of her skin, she found a way of darkening her skin with coffee. Mr. Walker was alone amongst other missionaries to approve her action. She did not need to change the colour of her eyes, of which she had bitterly complained when she was a child: they were already brown. Inspired by the Son of God who had shared human life to bring salvation, Amy wanted to share the life of the Indian people amongst whom she worked. Her dress enabled her to pass unnoticed in a temple in her search for children.

Years later, she was very moved when an Indian asked her whether she could show the people the life of her Lord Jesus. She had been asked the same questions back in her days in Japan. For Amy, the whole purpose of her life was to make the truth of the Gospel visible. Every action, every gesture, whether big or small, had to speak of the Kingdom. With the apostle Paul, she was convinced,

> *For through the law I died to the law, so that I might live to God. I have been crucified with Christ; and it is no longer I who live, but it is Christ who lives in me. And the life I now live in the flesh I live by faith in the Son of God, who loved me and gave himself for me (Gal. 2:19–20).*

In speaking of her activities, Amy would say that she was engaged in the 'King's Business'. She referred to it as 'K.B.'. She never wanted to do anything that might not be 'K.B.' and she used it as a criterion for judging what, and what not, to include in her day. Every morning, she would reflect on her programme. Which of the activities in her agenda would serve the Kingdom? Which would stand in the way of its progress? To the annoyance of many, she would refuse to attend meetings with colleagues if she felt they would do nothing to advance the work of the Kingdom, but was ready to walk for hours beneath the hot sun, along dusty roads, in order to rescue a single abandoned child. The community she founded at Dohnavur in 1901 quickly grew. By 1913, there were 130 young women. When the children were asked what attracted them to Amy, they would always answer that it was her love. By using 'K.B.' as her criterion, Amy had shown the children a mother's love: they called her 'Amma', which means 'Mummy'.

I often wonder how much we would grow in faith if we were to dare to look at our diaries the way Amy did. How much stronger would our testimony grow to be? In a modern culture in which many of us spend so much time dealing with all the information that is thrown at us, or keeping abreast of communications, do we ask ourselves what is really 'K.B.'? How might we be changed if, on a Monday morning, we looked at our diary and asked ourselves which of our activities most witnessed to the Kingdom? Our lifestyles can often be so fraught and pressurised as we run from one engagement to another, or so preoccupied by online activity, that we do not always take the time to ask the challenging questions.

Of course, working life can be very complicated, employers abusive, and the lists of tasks that are set before us may well be a far cry from a menu of Kingdom activities. Choices are often painfully hard to make. Colleagues can be difficult, budgets limited and work too burdensome to complete in the allotted time. Managers can lack understanding, while sometimes terms of contract go against the Kingdom values we hold to be precious.

Yet Emmanuel, God-with-us, shared our human life, in all its complexity. He remained faithful to the values of the Kingdom, and he invites his disciples to do the same. Everything counts in our testimony: the gesture of welcome we extend to others, whatever the colour of their skin or their sexual orientation, the smile of encouragement, the small kindness offered to a grieving colleague, the discrete act to lend someone a hand, the humble attitude shown towards the people we manage at work. In every place we go, Christ calls us to open our hearts to the yeast of the Kingdom and invites us to point with love and humility to the One whose authority takes priority over our lives.

Faithful and Committed Action

The Woman Who Anoints Jesus

Considering that Jesus' disciples have been following him for three years, it is surprising that they do not understand how the act of the woman announces both the Kingdom and the identity of Jesus. They are only capable of seeing the financial implications of what she does,

> *But when the disciples saw it, they were angry and said, "Why this waste? For this ointment could have been sold for a large sum, and the money given to the poor" (Matt. 26:8–9).*

They see the value of the *thing* rather than the meaning

of the *act*. Because of this, they are unable to see that the one among them is in need of it. Jesus tells them, "She has performed a good service for me. For you always have the poor with you" (Matt. 26:10–11).

For the disciples, the "poor" are the others, those who are absent, those who are somewhere else, who need to be the recipient of alms. They designate the "poor" by one single word, as they might talk about 'the sick', or 'the blind' or 'the lepers'. However, Jesus' response challenges and pushes his disciples to think again about their priorities, "… but you will not always have me" (Matt. 26:11).

These words of Jesus offer a contrast between 'the poor' understood as a whole group that exists in a general way somewhere else, and 'the person who is poor' who is right in front of them. The disciples speak of a moral duty towards 'the poor' in general, but are unable to recognise the face of the poor hidden in Jesus who,

> *… emptied himself,*
> *taking the form of a slave,*
> *being born in human likeness.*
> *And being found in human form (Phil. 2:7).*

> *For you know the generous act of our Lord Jesus*
> *Christ, that though he was rich, yet for your sakes he*
> *became poor, so that by his poverty you might become*
> *rich (2 Cor. 8:9).*

In the course of his ministry, on the other hand, Jesus recognises the particular need of each person who approaches him. Jesus reveals that the Kingdom does not exist just in theory, or simply as an intellectual concept, but is made known in everyday concrete actions that address the needs of each person: the deaf man, the mute boy, the sick girl, the fevered woman, the anxious father, the desperate mother, the rich young man, the poor widow.

As the woman pours her perfume over the head of Jesus, she demonstrates this concrete reality. She refuses to conform to the ways the disciples advocate for living faithfully. The Kingdom of God is not somewhere else, a hypothesis to be argued about or a moral obligation for another day. The yeast of the Kingdom of God is at work here and now, and now is the time to point to its Truth.

Jesus defends the woman's act against her critics. Amongst the latter is Judas. In the following episode, we find him in the act of betraying Jesus, "'What will you give me if I betray him to you?' They paid him thirty pieces of silver" (Matt. 26:15).

What a bitter contradiction! First, Judas is amongst those who are indignant that the perfume has not been sold to give the proceeds to the poor. Then, here he is immediately after, in the calculating process of obtaining huge riches for his personal profit. While Judas shows himself to be greedy, the woman offers what is precious. Judas' acts do nothing to serve the advance of the Kingdom. The woman's act, however, speaks of Jesus' true identity and points to a world built not on greed but on the values of God.

Amy Carmichael (cont'd)

When we come back to Amy's story, we find that, just like the woman who anoints Jesus, Amy was also confronted by criticism, especially the criticisms of those who did not understand what she was trying to do. She was increasingly aware that saving the individual children who came across her path, however important, was not everything. Other action was needed at a legislative level. She pursued her project with determination, approaching those who might be in a position to exert influence in a legal context. She was conscious of the pressing need for changes in the law to protect the lives of children. Reformers were at work in Calcutta and Bombay, so far without success. It was a very difficult area, fraught with problems.

On one occasion, she was invited to take part in a meeting with certain influential men. It was not an encouraging event. She wrote later,

> Two of the ten men were in earnest, the other eight enjoyed the talk preparatory and attendant upon all action in India, but they saw no tremendous reason for immediate exertion of any sort. The evil was decreasing: education, civilization, these elevating influences would gradually and pleasantly permeate society. In the meantime, we asked, what about the perishing children? Ah, it was sad, doubtless; that they should perish was indeed regrettable. But after all, were there many imperilled? For his part one old gentleman doubted it, though doubtless, he added cheerfully, unaware of the force of his admission, "a change in the law is much required."[51]

Influential people in the judiciary were not the only ones who failed to understand Amy's actions. Her readers and those who supported her in prayer and financially back home in Britain, too, struggled to do so. Throughout her ministry, Amy was deeply conscious that she depended on the prayer and the financial support of others. One day she received a word from the Lord to write what she

---
51   Elliot, *A Chance to Die*, 180.

had witnessed and when, sometime later, a missionary society asked her to write her experiences, she accepted the invitation as from God and set to work. She longed to explain in detail everything that was happening, so that those who supported her at home would have a better idea of her ministry and would be in a better position to pray.

Having spent hours writing about her ministry in India, hiding nothing of the situation of the children, she sent her manuscript off. It is not hard to imagine the surprise and disappointment she felt when the manuscript was refused! The Missionary Society considered that the text was too discouraging and strongly urged Amy to tone down what she had written and concentrate more on stories of success. She should render the content of her book less shocking and more positive. Undoubtedly, the society feared that if supporters read Amy's honest account, attendance at meetings would go down and financial support would dwindle. Frustrated and angry, Amy threw her manuscript into the depths of a drawer.

In 1900, two English friends came to visit Amy and saw everything that was happening with their own eyes. Discovering that the manuscript was still gathering dust where Amy had thrown it, they took it with them when they returned to Britain and managed to find a publisher. Embellished with the photographs that they themselves had taken, the book came out under the title, *Things as They Are*. Even though a preface talked of the exciting chapters that were hidden between the covers of the book, many readers were less than impressed. Where were the stories of all the great successes? The readers were keen to support the proclamation of the

Gospel, but were not clear that it was taking place in the life of this rather unusual missionary. Years later, Amy discovered that a committee of Christians in India had asked for her to be sent back to Britain. Her book had made disturbing reading.

Amy could certainly have returned home at that moment. She could have chosen a style of ministry that would have been less uncomfortable for those who supported her. However, she remained firm and threw herself even more passionately into her work. She had been suffering from poor health for some time, but would not allow it to get the better of her. Thanks to the efforts of others who confirmed the veracity of what she had written, Amy began to be accepted. In 1912, Queen Mary, the wife of George V and Empress of India, recognised the value of her work and offered the funding for a hospital. When Amy died in 1951, the law for the protection of children had been on the statute books for three years, even if the custom of temple prostitution persisted in some places. Amy's work had not been in vain.

Offering Our Actions to God

Amy Carmichael (cont'd)

Throughout her ministry, Amy had been wholly convinced that her purpose was not to please others, but to please God. Sometimes she was undoubtedly difficult to deal with. But Amy held firm. All her activities needed to be dedicated to God, even the most disagreeable and distasteful. In 1904, the community of Dohnavur—the 'Family'—consisted of 17 children, six of whom had been saved from prostitution. Amy always reminded her team of workers that the Lord had knelt down and washed the feet of his disciples. It was the task of the humblest slave. Amy was intent that the team should understand that no task was beneath their dignity. They were called to perform small and unpleasant tasks not because they were *women*, but because they were *followers of Christ*. They were there to take care of babies and children when the little ones fell ill. It was not always easy, especially as the sanitation and the state of the premises left a great deal to be desired. Yet during a visit to her daughter, Amy's mother described in a letter that it would have been difficult to find women, girls and babies more loving or more generous anywhere.

The team of women set to work, never shrinking from the most basic and distasteful jobs. It was a great testimony to the Kingdom in a culture in which activities were designated according to caste. The team members entrusted their work to God, in the faith that in his hands, each task was sanctified. If ever, before God, Amy wondered if it was really necessary to turn away from 'important' business in order to become mere nursemaids, the reply she received was always in the affirmative. The missionary understood that it was not the servant's role to choose between a small or a big task. She was called through all her actions to give expression to the love of Christ. She wrote later,

> If by doing some work which the undiscerning consider "not spiritual work" I can best help others, and I inwardly rebel, thinking it is the spiritual for

> which I crave, when in truth it is the interesting and exciting, then I know nothing of Calvary love.[52]

The Woman Who Anoints Jesus

In the same way as Amy offered up the small actions of her life to God, so the woman in our text also directs her act towards Jesus. Coming probably from a rich background, this woman takes great risks by coming into this house to find Jesus. Matthew tells us that this is the house of Simon the leper. Whoever Simon might be, what counts in Matthew's reference to him is that this house is associated with impurity, and Jesus enters it. We have already looked in Chapter IV at Jesus' relationship with those deemed ritually unclean. But here is a woman possibly putting her good reputation on the line by entering such a house.

Down the centuries, the woman's act, offered to Jesus, has often been interpreted as an image of worship. The outpoured perfume has been seen as a symbol of the heart of the worshipper, fully offered to God. It is certainly the case that in true worship, we offer our whole heart. But this fascinating episode, like the story of Amy Carmichael and those of countless other servants of God, encourages us to understand that it is not simply a matter of offering our whole selves at the moment of a church service. We are to offer ourselves in all activities, even in the most simple and humble. When we are aware of living in God's presence, an act offered in an attitude of prayer becomes the expression of real relationship with God. It becomes the outward sign of an inner reality.

In seeking the signs of the Kingdom more deeply in this moving story, we have found that the woman's act is charged

---
52 Amy Carmichael, *If* (Fort Washington, MD: CLC, 1938), 39.

with meaning. It is not simply a gesture of welcome, however generous it might be. It offers the image of the anointing of a king, and thereby speaks of Jesus' identity as the Messiah. The woman equally recognises by her act the mystery of sacrifice, present at the heart of the Kingdom. She prepares Jesus' body for burial. Her act points to the welcome of the Messiah of God who can only be fully recognised in his suffering and death.

The woman's act may be small, but it speaks of the greatness of the Kingdom, and stands in stark contrast to the actions of those who seek Jesus' arrest. The actions of these men, the enemies of Jesus, might be seen as significant and important on a human level, but in the end, they only express the smallness of human fears. Jesus affirms the value of this woman's humble and generous deed and shows that God receives with love the actions that we offer to him, however small they may be. He sees in them their eternal value.

Teachers affirm that children often learn better by being involved in a practical activity. Similarly, we may more easily remember what someone did than what they said. The proclamation of the Gospel is not accomplished simply in words, but must always be accompanied with action. After all, Jesus did not announce the Good News simply in words, but by his entire life, his death and resurrection. As the apostle Paul affirms, "Therefore just as one man's trespass led to condemnation for all, so one man's act of righteousness leads to justification and life for all" (Rom. 5:18).

Lord! ... Come in! Enter my small life! Lay your sacred hands on all the common things and small interests of that life and bless and change them. Transfigure my small resources, make them sacred. And in them give me your very self.
Evelyn Underhill [53]

---

53   (1875–1941), English mystic and theologian.

7. Giving All: The Transformative Kingdom

The more we become involved in the world,
the more we give ourselves to the world,
and the less we are of the world;
in truth,
what is of the world
does not give itself to the world.
Mother Maria Skobtsova[54]

Do not wish me out of this or in any way seek to get me out, for I will not be got out while this trial is on. These are my people, God has given them to me, and I will live or die for Him and His glory.
Gladys Aylward[55]

The action of yeast is nothing short of amazing. Mixed with flour and water, it starts to work and becomes, as if miraculously, a dynamic agent of change. At the end of the kneading process, the dough still seems fairly small. But before too long, it rises and swells, and in all its splendour is ready to

---

54 (1981–1945), Russian, orthodox religious in Paris, community builder, who died at Ravensbrück concentration camp for having resisted the Nazi regime.
55 (1902–1970), English-Chinese missionary in China.

be put in the oven. The change that has taken place is already remarkable.

However, for the dough to become bread, it has to be baked. During this process, the yeast, which has been so very much alive and active in the earlier process, has to die. It cannot survive at a high temperature. By the time the bread comes out of the oven, the yeast has not only done its work: it has been extinguished.

The yeast reminds us of the mysterious and extraordinary ways of the Kingdom of God. Unlike the kingdoms of this world, which are often built on consumerism, money and power, it is founded on love and self-giving. The pathway to the Kingdom leads from the transformation of humankind, through a life lived in obedience to God, right to the Cross.

The nature of true sacrifice that lies at the heart of God's Kingdom is revealed to us by Christ crucified. Unlike the violence inflicted upon victims of domestic abuse or upon so many young men compelled by their governments to go to war and 'sacrifice' themselves for their country, the sacrifice at the heart of the Kingdom is never forced. Rather, it is a free offering of the heart, in response to the God of the Gospel who chooses to love us freely. He has given himself fully and freely in Christ, and offers to humankind the freedom to love in return.

In baptism, the Christian is identified with the death and resurrection of Christ. This is the great and profound mystery of the Kingdom,

> *For through the law I died to the law, so that I might live to God. I have been crucified with Christ; and it is no longer I who live, but it is Christ who lives in me. And the life I now live in the flesh I live by faith in the Son of God, who loved me and gave himself for me (Gal. 2:19–20).*

The Mother of James and John (Matt. 20:20–28; 27:55–56)

Even though the story of James' and John's mother takes up relatively little space in Matthew's Gospel, I find it both fascinating and inspiring. We meet her for the first time when she is on the road to Jerusalem, where her exchange with Jesus is presented centre-stage.

> *Then the mother of the sons of Zebedee came to him with her sons, and kneeling before him, she asked a favor of him. And he said to her, "What do you want?" She said to him, "Declare that these two sons of mine will sit, one at your right hand and one at your left, in your kingdom." But Jesus answered, "You do not know what you are asking. Are you able to drink the cup that I am about to drink?" They said to him, "We are able." He said to them, "You will indeed drink my cup, but to sit at my right hand and at my left, this is not mine to grant, but it is for those for whom it has been prepared by my Father."*
>
> *When the ten heard it, they were angry with the two brothers. But Jesus called them to him and said, "You know that the rulers of the Gentiles lord it over them, and their great ones are tyrants over them. It will not be so among you; but whoever wishes to be great among you must be your servant, and whoever wishes to be first among you must be your slave; just as the Son of Man came not to be served but to serve, and to give his life a ransom for many" (Matt. 20:20–28).*

Following this episode, the next time we meet her is at the scene of the crucifixion,

> Many women were also there, looking on from a distance; they had followed Jesus from Galilee and had provided for him. Among them were Mary Magdalene, and Mary the mother of James and Joseph, and the mother of the sons of Zebedee (Matt. 27:55–56).

If we were to scan these verses over with a hurried eye, we might be tempted to retell her story in this way,

> The mother of James and John has great ambitions for her sons. As ignorant of the Kingdom's values as she is pretentious, she approaches Jesus one day and unashamedly asks him to select them for leading roles in his administration when he comes to power. Jesus' response to her shows that she understands nothing of the nature of his ministry, and he painstakingly has to repeat a lesson that he has already given before (Matt. 18:1–6). Together with a number of other women who take care of Jesus, this woman just happens to be present at the scene of Jesus' death.

However, if we approach this passage more carefully, reading it in search of signs of the transformation that lies at the heart of the Kingdom, we make amazing discoveries about the life of this courageous and dynamic woman of faith. Her discipleship is one that grows and develops beyond recognition as she follows Jesus.

The Beginning: Lots to Learn

The mother of James and John reasons in the same way as many parents. She wants the very best for her children. The wife of a fisherman, she dares to hope that one day her sons will reach a higher social standing than that of their father. She would so love them to be well respected one day and looked up to by others. In coming to Jesus and asking for high positions for her sons, she undoubtedly imagines that if Jesus has chosen them to belong to the Twelve, and—even better—to be among the three favourites alongside Peter (Matt. 17:1), they must be in line for an impressive promotion sometime soon.

In expressing her ambition for her children, she also gives voice to her own. At the time of Jesus, the social position of a woman normally depended on that occupied by the father of the family. Before marriage, a daughter was dependent on her father. As a wife, she was dependent on her husband and as a widow, on her sons or other male relative. Given that the principal purpose of a woman at the time was thought to be to bear children to her husband, she was rarely referred to by her own name, but more often identified by her family relationships. It is unsurprising, therefore, that in this first episode, Matthew never calls her by her name. He does not even describe her as the mother of James and John. In the thinking of the ancient world, she is the wife of Zebedee and the *mother of her husband's sons*.

With the exception of rich widows or women belonging to the higher echelons of society, women rarely had the opportunity to forge their own standing in society wholly by their own independent competence. When this mother asks for places for her sons in Jesus' coming Kingdom, she probably hopes that she will share their glory. She longs to see her sons become rich and famous, revered by the people. Perhaps she dreams of splendid palaces and magnificent chariots.

In talking about the "Kingdom" of Jesus, the wife of Zebedee may well be imagining a political or geographical territory. As we have already established, first-century Israel lived under Roman occupation. The presence of Roman military aroused feelings in the population of hatred and distrust. The people of Israel knew only too well from their own experience how the leaders of the Gentiles could 'lord it over the nations'. Certain people, and perhaps the mother of James and John was among them, looked forward to the day when the nation of Israel was free to become a powerful political power once more. Not everyone belonged to a resistance group, as Simon the Zealot (Matt. 10:4) may well have done. However, a large number of people shared the desire to see their nation freed from occupation and looked back with pride to the reign of King David. Matthew describes the indignation of the disciples of Jesus when they hear this mother's request. It may well be that they are less shocked by the stupidity of her request than filled with jealousy: they, too, would like to occupy positions of power one day.

However, Jesus' plans for his disciples are a million miles away from this woman's dreams. Jesus explains that the Kingdom of God does not resemble the kingdoms of this world. Its ways are fundamentally different, founded on the divine values of service and self-giving that, inseparably, express outwardly the inner attitude of humble obedience to God, "... the Son of Man came not to be served but to serve, and to give his life a ransom for many" (Matt. 20:28).

Jesus' words "serve" and "give himself", remind us of the description of the Suffering Servant prophesied by Isaiah. This servant, in perfect obedience to God, undergoes the suffering and death that others deserve,

> *See, my servant shall prosper;*
> *he shall be exalted and lifted up,*
> *and shall be very high.*

> *... he had no form or majesty that we should look at him,*
> *nothing in his appearance that we should desire him.*
> *He was despised and rejected by others;*

> *a man of suffering and acquainted with infirmity;*
> *and as one from whom others hide their faces*
> *he was despised, and we held him of no account.*
>
> *Surely he has borne our infirmities*
> *and carried our diseases;*
> *yet we accounted him stricken,*
> *struck down by God, and afflicted.*
> *But he was wounded for our transgressions,*
> *crushed for our iniquities;*
> *upon him was the punishment that made us whole,*
> *and by his bruises we are healed.*
> *All we like sheep have gone astray;*
> *we have all turned to our own way,*
> *and the Lord has laid on him*
> *the iniquity of us all.*
>
> *He was oppressed, and he was afflicted,*
> *yet he did not open his mouth;*
> *like a lamb that is led to the slaughter,*
> *and like a sheep that before its shearers is silent,*
> *so he did not open his mouth.*
> *By a perversion of justice he was taken away.*
> *Who could have imagined his future?*
> *For he was cut off from the land of the living,*
> *stricken for the transgression of my people.*
> *They made his grave with the wicked*
> *and his tomb with the rich,*
> *although he had done no violence,*
> *and there was no deceit in his mouth*
> *(Is. 52:13; 53:2b–9).*

In our discussion of Peter's mother-in-law, we saw how

Matthew considers God's perfect servant to be the one who brings healing. However, in recounting Jesus' conversation with the mother of James and John, Matthew implies that obedience to God will lead Jesus much further. The cross of Jesus will not only be the result of injustice and the sinful outworking of violent human systems. It will also be the fulfilment of Isaiah's prophecy and the ultimate expression of humble service lived according to the values of the Kingdom of God.

Up until this moment in the Gospel story, we have not even heard of the mother of James and John. Matthew is introducing her for the very first time when he portrays her coming to Jesus to ask for places of glory for her sons. At this point, she still has a great deal to learn. If we were to close our Bibles and not take the trouble to read further on, we might very likely be left with rather a negative impression of this woman. We might retain from our reading only the caricature of an ambitious mother, who has not the slightest clue of what the Kingdom of God is really about.

If we keep our Bibles open and read right on to the end of the Gospel story, however, we learn that this very same mother is present amongst a group of women who have been faithful to Jesus all the way through, since the time of his ministry in Galilee. We might have imagined that once Jesus refused her request, she just slunk away like the rich young ruler (Matt. 19:16–22) and went back home disappointed and cynical. If Jesus did not intend to give places of honour to her sons, why stay with him? Yet, the Gospel story announces, startlingly, that she continues to follow Jesus all the way to Jerusalem and is even present at the moment of his death. What an extraordinary journey! She grows to be a fully-fledged woman of the Kingdom.

But what in the life of this woman has prepared her to be a witness of Jesus' death? What elements of the Kingdom have been present in her life, encouraging her and enabling her to grow in faith and understanding? If we spend a moment looking carefully at the words Matthew has chosen to describe this woman we might find the answer to our question.

First Element of Transformation: Learning to Follow Jesus

It turns out that, together with other women, the mother of James and John has been following Jesus since the early stages of his ministry. The word 'follow' occupies a crucial place in the language and thinking of the Gospel. At the very beginning of the Gospel story, Jesus comes into Galilee and announces that "the Kingdom of heaven has come near" (Matt. 4:17). He issues a call to repentance (Matt. 4:17). Then, the very first action of Jesus is to call disciples. When he sees Simon and Andrew, he pronounces the essential invitation, *"Follow me"*. A few verses later, when Jesus calls James and John, the same key word appears again (Matt. 4:22). The invitation to *follow* is the fundamental call of Jesus (Matt. 8:22; 9:9) in addressing his disciples. By *following* their leader, the disciples become apprentices of the Kingdom, whose values are made known in the life, death and resurrection of Jesus.

The Gospels remind us over and again that Christian life is not solely a matter of believing that Christ died for us on the cross. Christian commitment is much more than confessing our sin and receiving the forgiveness of God. It is all about *following* Jesus, living in imitation of Jesus in all the many contexts of our everyday life. If we are to learn the values of the Kingdom, there is no better way to do so than to follow the one whose life fully and abundantly demonstrated them. In the company of Jesus, we learn to love, pray and forgive, to cross divides and offer space to welcome the outcast. We learn to denounce injustice, serving and persevering and offering ourselves in trust to God, not knowing where he will lead us.

We shall be gradually changed and sanctified as we follow.

The Future God Has in Store for Us

Matthew describes how, in responding to the call of Jesus, Simon and Andrew leave their nets (Matt. 4:20). Their life changes. They have, no doubt, been in the fishing business since their early years. Moreover, they probably expected to be fishermen all their lives, considering that sons were expected to follow their father at this time. (Jesus himself learnt a carpenter's trade.) Jesus' invitation to follow, however, overturns all their plans and expectations. Their desire to follow Jesus compels them to leave a predictable future behind them and launch out on a deeper path that will lead them towards God's future—one they do not yet see.

I cannot help but smile when I read Jesus' words to Simon the fisherman, as he throws his net into the water,

> *And he said to them, "Follow me, and I will make you fish for people" (Matt. 4:19).*

Peter will one day play the primary role in the life of the early Church. After the resurrection and ascension of Jesus, he becomes the 'fisher of men' that Jesus had once promised. As a man who started out in the fish business, he had acquired a host of skills essential for catching fish and surviving on the lake. He had learnt patience and perseverance when fish were slow to come, to say nothing of the courage necessary to face a storm. He had learnt to react quickly in response to danger. As a missionary of the early Church, God will put all these skills and talents to use. Nothing of Peter will be lost. Following Jesus, Peter will still be a fisherman, but for God. He will need patience and perseverance to announce the Gospel. He will need courage to face tribunals and to endure arrest and imprisonment. In the course of the development of the early Church, Peter will resemble Jesus more and more, while becoming more and more truly himself. It will be an extraordinary transformation.

The life of James and John changes in the same way. We read that these brothers leave "their boat and their father". This is a stupendous decision. At the time of Jesus, all family members were to live in submission to their father. Yet, here are two fishermen getting up and *leaving* their father. Taking the decision to follow Jesus, their lives recognise a higher authority: that of God the Father. They commit themselves to living according to the values of their new master—to the values of the Kingdom.

From the moment that we set out on the road, following Jesus, the doors of our life open out into a new future—the one that God has in store. Our horizons grow wider. Our perspectives grow deeper. We begin to be moulded and kneaded by the hands of the Baker. This road will take us on a long journey, even though, to begin with, we do not know where or in which direction.

When the women set out to follow Jesus in Galilee, they also make an extraordinary decision, arguably greater than the one made by the men. They break with the norms of their society and, in leaving home, turn their back on the traditional household. These women cannot guess that their faith will lead them to follow Jesus all the way to Jerusalem—the great city. They cannot predict that one day they will hear the baying of the crowd or witness, close-up, the corruption of the judicial system. They certainly do not imagine that one day they will watch while the death penalty is meted out to one they love.

None of the Christians whose stories we have told so far in this book could imagine in their youth where God would lead them in years to come. The more faithful they were to Christ, the more deeply they were prepared for the tasks to come later. In working in Ireland and in England amongst mill workers, Amy Carmichael was unaware that this was preparing her for a ministry in Japan. Once there, she could not guess that her later years would be spent in South India working amongst abandoned children. Similarly, at the time of her conversion, Sabina could not know that she would be working amongst handicapped people one day. Corrie ten Boom, whom we shall meet in the next chapter, expresses it this way,

> I know that the experiences of our lives, when we let God use them, become the mysterious and perfect preparation for the work He will give us to do.[56]

Alice Domon

Another woman who did not guess what was in store for her was the French missionary, Alice Domon (1937–1977). Setting out for Argentina in 1967 as a young religious, she had no idea of the ministry or martyrdom to which she would be called. She wrote to her family three months after leaving Toulouse. Despite her feelings of not being up to the task, she had begun her ministry in teaching, but already had the sense that God might lead her somewhere else,

> I hardly feel qualified to teach … I would much rather dedicate myself to evangelisation. It really interests me, I enjoy relating to people.[57]

---

56   Corrie ten Boom, John Sherrill and Elizabeth Sherrill, *The Hiding Place* (London, UK: Hodder & Stoughton, 1971), p. 20.
57   Diana Beatriz Viñoles, *Lettres d'Alice Domon: Une disparue d'Argentine* (Paris: Karthala, 2016), p. 27.

> Looking at things from a 'beginner's' point of view, she felt suited to the work of evangelisation. She had not the faintest inkling of how God would put her startling relational abilities to use. Neither did she have any idea of the extent to which she herself would be 'evangelised': transformed by the Gospel, imbued with the values of the Kingdom, and sanctified more and more as she followed Christ.

Heady First Days

According to Matthew, the group of women who have followed Jesus will have experienced the wonderful, crowd-drawing, heady days of his ministry in Galilee. At the beginning of his ministry, Jesus attracts crowds wherever he goes, all eager to listen to his teaching or to ask for healing. Those in his company bask in reflected glory. When they go from village to village across Galilee, they listen to his teaching surrounded by audiences of thousands. What a delight to see their master surrounded by people in need asking for help. How proud they are when they see his reputation spread far and wide. Certainly, Jesus already has his opponents, but nonetheless the disciples can feel satisfied that they are following a master who has become widely celebrated.

Alice Domon (cont'd)

Alice Domon also experienced a honeymoon period at the beginning of her ministry. She felt that there were encouraging signs everywhere she looked,

> [These people] haven't suffered as a result of the

> war, it's a whole new world moving confidently forward, they want to find out about their world and change it. You can't imagine how hungry they are for God, and everything to do with him. The traditions are just amazing![58]
>
> In the poor parish of Villa Lugano, a shantytown where she went on Sundays, Alice was equally encouraged,
>
> The chapel is so small, it's bursting at the seams ... the parish is full of life, the people are really nice, friendly and dynamic.[59]

It is almost always a pleasure to find ourselves in a church building that is full to bursting and to experience church community that is full of life. It encourages and energises us; the warmth of the fellowship seems to surround us like a comforting blanket. Living in such an environment, however, is not always the sign that we have arrived at a mature point of spiritual development. On the contrary, it may be that God has something else in store for us elsewhere.

Transformed by Following

The Gospel of Matthew reminds us that the disciples' experience following their master in Galilee is not an end in itself: they are being prepared to go further. They will be called to cross other thresholds and meet other challenges. This is undoubtedly true of the women. When we encounter them

---

58   Viñoles, *Lettres d'Alice Domon*, 26.
59   Viñoles, *Lettres d'Alice Domon*, 37–38.

watching the crucifixion of Jesus, we know that these women must have followed Jesus not just during the heady days of the Galilean ministry, but also on the road to Jerusalem. They would also have been listening in as Jesus' teaching has grown increasingly deep and challenging. The nearer they get to the great city, the more difficult and uncomfortable the teaching becomes for those who receive it. Addressing his disciples, Jesus sets out the great challenge,

> *If any want to become my followers, let them deny themselves and take up their cross and follow me (Matt. 16:24).*

Suddenly new horizons open up for Jesus' listeners. Up until now, nothing has been too difficult. There has been a certain ease and even a kind of 'benefit' in following Jesus: crowds, fame, welcome. They could not have dreamed of more. But suddenly, there is a shift. Following Jesus has other implications: self-denial, self-giving; a risky business. Taking up a cross? It could mean humility, not to say humiliation, suffering, even death.

Alice Domon (cont'd)

For Alice too, new challenges were opening up. Not unlike the women who follow Jesus from Galilee, the more Alice advanced on the road to the Kingdom, the more she began to realise how deep the challenge of Jesus' teaching really was. Desiring to be more obedient to the Gospel, she took the decision to leave the relatively comfortable and secure environment of the mission house to live in the shantytown. Other sisters in her congregation made a similar choice. It was a brave and adventurous decision that broke the mould of usual practice. Alice had committed herself to following the Son of God and she wanted her life to be open to him. Believing that Jesus had renounced glory to share human life, Alice sought to follow him faithfully by sharing her life more fully with the people to whom she had been sent. She wrote,

> It's costly to give up a comfortable, rather well-off life-style, and swap it for the sort of life that the Lord lived in Palestine amongst the people of his time ... he alone can teach us, provided we are ready to listen.[60]

What a change had already taken place in the life of this young missionary! Like other women living in the shantytown, she found a part-time job as a cleaner, and this freed her to be of service to others for the rest of the day. It was a road of discovery for her. Living this way enabled her not only to witness the struggles of the everyday lives of the people around her, but to share it more fully,

> [I'm writing] from the hospital where I'm looking after a little mite—one of these little 2-month old kids who weighs 2.5 kilos. He has nothing but a wide-open mouth in his face and a big swollen tummy, and large, sad eyes full of questions. He hasn't even got the strength to cry when he's hungry. He's a total image for our oppressed people ... [T]oday he's turned a corner and the doctors are saying he'll get better. The worst thing is that in a

---

60   Viñoles, *Lettres d'Alice Domon*, 99.

few months the same thing will happen all over again. We'll have to find somewhere else for him because his parents haven't the wherewithal to take care of him properly.[61]

Dramatic as it already was, Alice's transformation did not stop here. The more poverty and injustice she saw, the more she was drawn to active commitment. She started to support a network of militants campaigning for the installation of public services in the shantytowns. She helped with the administration, wrote letters, and sometimes looked after the children of people who needed to attend meetings. This movement achieved concrete results, such as the introduction of a water supply in certain areas.

Meanwhile, her faith was becoming deeper and she was giving of herself in more costly ways. There was a family living not far from where she and a nurse were sharing a house. Both the parents and the children were frequently falling ill because they lived so near the rubbish tip. Alice and her nurse colleague bravely took the decision to swap houses with the family. When a friend of theirs came to visit them in their new accommodation, she was deeply moved. She wrote later,

> I found them covered with bites, because the door was made of canvas and the dogs were getting in and sleeping beside them. It was the poorest thing I ever saw.[62]

Alice had left her refrigerator behind her in the other

---

61 Viñoles, *Lettres d'Alice Domon*, 96.
62 Pierron, *Missionnaire sous la dictature*, 22.

> house so that the family could use it. Installed in her new accommodation, she desired to have no material possession that the poorest people did not have. Increasingly transformed by the values of the Kingdom, she wanted to share their life fully. One day a number of her neighbours were arrested and never returned. Alice only increased her efforts, perhaps not thinking that one day she might disappear like them.

Alice's transformation reminds us that we cannot set out to follow Jesus and expect to stay the same. Our transformation is a long-term project. Christian life is not a matter of a single moment of change, at the time of taking a decision for Christ or at the time of being confirmed or baptised as a believer. As Christians, we are called to live in a continuous and progressive process of change. Every day, we are called to turn around and offer ourselves to the one who, by the power of the Holy Spirit, will always take us further. With spiritual maturity, Christian life does not become easier and easier. Rather it grows richer and deeper, provided—as Alice wrote—"we are ready to listen to him".

Second Element of Transformation: Learning to Serve

Let us turn back to the Gospel of Matthew. In speaking of the women who have followed Jesus, Matthew affirms that they have also "served". The two key words of the Gospel, "follow" and "serve" are side by side in this verse. By his choice of language, Matthew suggests that these women have grasped the profound meaning of life with Jesus.

We have already reflected on the theme of service in Chapter III, when we looked at the story of Peter's mother-in-law. We should not be too surprised to find that the word Matthew used to describe the service of Peter's mother-in-law is the same word that he uses to speak of the faithfulness of the women following Jesus. It is also the word that Jesus uses to describe the call of the Son of Man.

The extraordinary truth is that the mother of James and John has become one of the women who have followed and served. This is the proof that she has finally begun to grasp the teaching of her master. There was a time when she was ambitious for her sons and herself, and anxious to climb the greasy pole of the social ladder. However, the yeast of the Kingdom has been at work within her. In stark contrast to the behaviour of her very own sons, who flee at the moment of Jesus' arrest, this woman remains faithful to the last and witnesses the death of Jesus on the cross.[63]

Transformed by Serving

As disciples of Christ, we cannot follow him without being dramatically changed by the service to which he calls us. The whole business of serving engages us in a new vision of society and a different way of looking at others. Matthew tells how the mother of James and John, together with other women, watch the death of Jesus from a distance. She does not shut her eyes to the suffering of her Lord, nor is her presence near the cross just a matter of briefly catching sight of what is happening. No, these women have made the decision to have their eyes wide open. Theirs is an honest and courageous watching.

We know from our own experience how difficult it is to watch others suffer, especially our loved ones. We know the

---

[63] Some traditions suggest that "the beloved disciple" who appears beneath the cross in John's Gospel (John 19:26) was John the apostle. However, John's Gospel never explicitly identifies "the beloved disciple" with this John, and his identity remains a mystery hotly debated by scholars. Matthew's Gospel never mentions him.

horror and agony of going to hospital to visit a child who is desperately ill, or the sorrow and pain of visiting the mother or father who can no longer recognise who we are. And here, at the end of Matthew's Gospel, is this mother, once ambitious for her sons, ready to be associated with a crucified prisoner and accompany his suffering.

The faithfulness of this woman takes her outside the city walls. At the place of the Skull, the mother of James and John witnesses the horror and injustice of crucifixion. She sees and hears it all: the soldiers, the bandits crucified beside Jesus, the passers-by, the scribes and the elders, the high-priests, the centurion. But of course, she does not look on it all with an objective eye, nor does she see events from the point of view of the executioners or the madding crowd. All these perspectives demand the death of Jesus. Rather, this faithful woman observes all that happens from the point of view of the suffering one.

She hears the insults directed at him as wounds rather than as taunts. She situates the two other bandits in relation to where Jesus is—one on his right and one on his left—and perhaps remembers that she had once asked Jesus to give places of honour to her sons: one on his right and one on his left. She had imagined such places to be situations of glory. But by following and serving Jesus, this woman has been totally changed. Her perceptions, priorities and values are no longer the same. Not long before, she was pretentious and hungry for glory. Now, here, she sees the world through the eyes of the crucified one.

Alice Domon (cont'd)

Back in Argentina, Alice Domon also had her perceptions changed by following and serving Christ. Like the mother of James and John, Alice Domon also became a witness of suffering and injustice. In 1973, Alice moved from the shantytown Villa Lugano to Perrugoria in the North-East of Argentina. She had heard of the Agrarian League operating in the north of Argentina and wanted to support the increasing numbers of those experiencing crippling poverty and who were fighting for their rights. This new region offered further insights into the suffering of the country people. As the political situation became tenser and more dangerous, so their poverty increased. In her letters to her family, Alice spoke less and less about herself. She decreasingly wrote of 'me' and increasingly of 'us'. She understood herself as one of the people.

> Heat, hunger and illness often eat away at *us*, but *we* believe that it's together that *we* must find a way out of *our* poverty. ... medicine costs a fortune, and only the rich can afford to be ill here. The other day we [came to the hospital], three small kids and their mum, on one horse there was the mum with two of the kids, [3 and 6 months] and then me on the other horse with a six-year old girl. By the time we got to the hospital the sun was beating down on us and the heat was terrible, *our* kids had fallen asleep on the way, and the doctor wasn't there, I tell you we could have wept to have to turn back in the same heat, but there was no point crying—we just had to put a brave face on it and come home again, but with the temperature at 40° we had to wait until 4 o'clock at the sisters' house and then eventually got to the farm just as the sun was going down.[64]

---

64 Viñoles, *Lettres d'Alice Domon*, 132–133, emphasis mine.

> Sharing the suffering of the people, Alice affirmed the presence of Christ who, himself, knew suffering,

> We believe that the Lord is present in the midst of this suffering, that he is making himself known, and that, as committed Christians, we must be watchful.[65]

Alice was coming more and more to grasp the meaning of Jesus' teaching. In another parable in Matthew's Gospel, Jesus affirms that those who will inherit the life of the Kingdom will be the ones who give themselves in service to the very poorest of the world,

> *Then the king will say to those at his right hand, "Come, you that are blessed by my Father, inherit the kingdom prepared for you from the foundation of the world; for I was hungry and you gave me food, I was thirsty and you gave me something to drink, I was a stranger and you welcomed me, I was naked and you gave me clothing, I was sick and you took care of me, I was in prison and you visited me" (Matt. 25:34–36).*

Through this parable, Jesus invites his listeners to seek and recognise his image in the face of those in need. Jesus offers a list not just of those who suffer, but of those who for him are the most insignificant, the most invisible and most outcast of society,

> *And the king will answer them, "Truly I tell you, just as you did it to one of the least of these who are members of my family, you did it to me" (Matt. 25:40).*

---

65   Viñoles, *Lettres d'Alice Domon*, 131.

Jesus invites his disciples to recognise his image also in the faces of children, who at the time were considered the very least in society. As Jesus says, "Whoever welcomes one such child in my name welcomes me" (Matt. 18:5).

To what extent does our faithfulness to Christ lead us to see him in those who suffer? These passages invite us to recognise the presence of Christ in the victims of poverty, of war, of injustice of all kinds. Very often, anaesthetised by the values of our surrounding culture, we are tempted to establish our priorities and make our choices solely on the basis of our own interests or those of our immediate family. Perhaps in such moments, we are not unlike the mother of James and John, who asks for benefits for her own sons.

Christ calls us, however, to submit our choices to the sovereignty of God. The values of the Kingdom must inform the way we live, hope, pray, vote, spend our money and imagine the future. The women present at the cross remind us, as Alice does, that the more closely we follow Jesus, the more we are transformed by the Kingdom's values. We are called to open our eyes wide and have the courage to see Christ amongst the poorest people, be they on the other side of the world or just on the other side of the street.

Third Element of Transformation: Faithfulness to the End

Let us return again briefly to the mother of James and John. In stark contrast to the apostles, she does not flee. She does not hide behind locked doors in a house somewhere, nor does she seek other possible avenues for expressing her faithfulness to Jesus. She remains. At Golgotha, she stands sufficiently near the cross to see. (The Romans did not permit spectators to stand close to a cross.) Just as Joseph of Arimathea will approach Pilate and ask for the body of Jesus (Matt. 27:57–58), this woman is willing to associate herself publically with the crucified one, making herself vulnerable both to arrest, and to the violence of the soldiers. Jesus was right when he said that those who followed him should take up *their* cross.

Alice Domon (cont'd)

Alice Domon demonstrated the same fidelity. She stayed put in a situation that put her in danger. Sometime after her move to Perrugoria, she took the courageous decision to resign from her congregation. Other sisters also working in Argentina decided similarly. It was an unusual step, to say the least. Alice rejected all possibility of being protected by an institution, and had no wish to be called back to France by a superior understandably anxious for her safety. It was an extraordinary act of faith, taking her in a direction of which she would probably never have dreamed when she first set out. She was committed to sharing the life of her fellow countrymen and women, and to sharing the dangers that they experienced.

In 1976, following a further military coup that took power in Argentina, Alice had to leave Perugorria. In the course of the following year, some twenty people from the village disappeared, including leaders of the Agrarian League and villagers who had welcomed Alice into their house. Some disappeared or were imprisoned. Alice first went further north where she worked very long days in the cotton fields for a pittance so small she barely had enough to buy food, then journeyed to Buenos Aires. She brought the wives of the disappeared villagers to Buenos Aires so that they could pursue their search for their lost loved ones in the capital city. So far, they had received no news of the husbands.

In the capital, Alice got in touch with the Mothers

of the Plaza da Mayo and became involved with one of the groups. During this time of violent repression in Argentina, the mothers of kidnapped people gathered together regularly to offer mutual support. Their children had been captured and taken away in the middle of night, disappeared without trace. The authorities had never offered any explanation or information. The women had no idea of the reasons for their loved ones' disappearance nor where they were imprisoned, not even whether they were alive or dead. They had done the rounds of the prisons, hospitals and military bases; they had pleaded their case before judges and government officials. Nothing.

While these mothers had initially met to support one another, they eventually began to organise. On Thursdays, they assembled in Buenos Aires in the public square in front of the Ministry for Home Affairs, and became known the world over for their silent vigil. Numbers grew as they confronted the silence of oppressive power with the silence of love. Many of them were threatened, attacked or removed in the same way that their children had been. Standing alongside the mothers in faith, Alice had made the decision not to leave. Recognising that the Church was being called into unknown territory as it stood with those who faced oppression, Alice accompanied the mothers in their research. She saw the presence of the crucified Christ reflected in their experience,

> ... the anguish of the mothers searching for their kidnapped children, all the suffering and the ways of the Cross they walk through government dens and police stations etc. ... This is the passion that

so many families are experiencing today to say nothing of the torture so many people are enduring in prisons and elsewhere ... Let us beseech the Lord to grant us his strength and his light.[66]

Alice continued to offer support to the mothers and to help them at an organisational level. Not long after a demonstration in front of the Congress building, she was arrested and detained for 24 hours. Conscious of the dangers, she sought in her letters to reassure her family back home. However, in December 1977, she was present at a meeting of the parents of the disappeared in one of the churches. The group was seeking to publish an article in a newspaper demanding the truth about the disappeared. As she came out of the meeting, Alice was arrested along with some ten other women. They had been betrayed by a new member of the group, an infiltrator, who had claimed to be seeking a lost brother. The following day Léonie Duquet, one of Alice's colleagues, was also arrested. All these women were taken to the biggest concentration camp in Buenos Aires. Faithful to her Saviour unto death, Alice was tortured before being thrown from an aircraft, drugged and still alive, into the depths of the ocean.

In 2010, Alice's youngest sister was a witness at the trial of ESMA, the organisation responsible for the disappearance and murder of Alice and all those like her. "Perhaps it was, arguably, subversive to want dignity for the poor," she said of Alice. "But really what underpinned her action was her faith."[67] In her last letter to her family, Alice wrote, "it is remarkable how suffering can make

---

66 Viñoles, *Lettres d'Alice Domon*, 166.
67 Montoya Angeline, *la famille Domon*.

> people grow—as much as it can destroy them."⁶⁸ Although she was not speaking of herself, Alice was undoubtedly one of those people who, through her faithfulness to Christ, grew as she shared the suffering of those who were destroyed by it. This faithful disciple was prepared to follow her Lord and carry her cross, even if it meant making the supreme sacrifice.

The witness of both the mother of James and John, and of Alice Domon, have spoken powerfully of the action of the yeast, secretly at work to transform the dough through and through. We have watched, amazed, as the mother of James and John has been changed from being the parent whose sole motivation is the well-being of her own children, to the disciple who is ready to put all at risk, daring to witness the agony of Jesus when his other followers have run away.⁶⁹ Her witness to Jesus invites us to journey more deeply into the mystery of the Kingdom of God.

Meanwhile, we have accompanied Alice as she has walked the way of the Cross. We have watched her as she journeyed from teaching those with learning difficulties, into the service of the inhabitants of a shantytown, then of country people exploited by their masters, and finally of the mothers of the disappeared. We have seen how she was changed as she shared their poverty, their suffering and their struggles. We have witnessed her transformation from the young religious she was on her arrival, enjoying the warmth of a lively parish, into the mature disciple she became, ready to break the mould and take highly unconventional steps of faith, thus making herself as vulnerable as those whose life she shared. Alice had

---

68   Viñoles, *Lettres d'Alice Domon*, 167.
69   See note 63 on page 187.

written, "I have chosen to live with and for them". However, by making this commitment, Alice was effectively committing herself, should she be called, to die "with and for them". As she followed Christ and gave herself to God more and more in the service of others, she was transformed to the point of becoming herself one of the disappeared.

If in our preceding chapters, we have spoken of the adventure of faith, in this chapter we have begun to see the path along which the adventurers might just be led to walk. The two women we have looked at in this chapter have enabled us to see how we can be changed when we follow Christ faithfully along the road. As the mother of James and John exemplified, it is never too late to learn the great truths of the Kingdom of God. We are never too old. God may lead us to places we never imagined possible, "provided," as Alice said, "we are ready to listen to him."

8 LIVING HOPEFULLY: THE PROMISED KINGDOM

If I could give you information of my life, it would be to show how a very ordinary ability has been led by God in strange and unaccustomed paths, to do in His service what He has done in her. And if I could tell you all, you would see how God has done all, and I nothing.
Florence Nightingale[70]

But because I am a woman, ought I therefore to believe that I should not tell you of the goodness of God, when I saw at the same time that it is his will that it should be known?
Julian of Norwich[71]

In depicting a woman in the process of making bread, this parable projects us into the future. Yes, the narrative of the parable itself stops at the point when the dough is fully mixed. But it is impossible not to think of the rest of the story: the baking, the serving and the sharing; the appetising smell wafting out from the oven and the delicious moment of biting into the fresh, warm softness of the bread. From start to finish, this woman's intention is as visionary as it is generous: the

---

70 (1820–1910), English nurse and medical reformer.
71 (1342–c1415), Medieval English anchoress and first woman writer in English. Julian, *Showings* (Mahwah, NJ: Paulist Press, 1977), p. 285.

loaf will be enormous! In taking three measures of flour, the woman is preparing not just enough bread for her family, but for a whole crowd of people with empty stomachs. The action of the yeast on these three measures will make the already large quantity of flour even greater.

Pointing forwards, the parable has a meaning not just for today but for tomorrow as well. It reminds us that the Kingdom of God, already at work in 'all the dough', will continue to be active until the end of time. Then, in the great and beautiful purposes of God, it will be celebrated in all its splendour at a banquet to which all the people of the earth are invited,

> *On this mountain the Lord of hosts will make*
> *for all peoples*
> *a feast of rich food, a feast of well-aged wines,*
> *of rich food filled with marrow, of well-aged wines*
> *strained clear.*
> *... he will swallow up death forever.*
> *Then the Lord God will wipe away the tears from all*
> *faces,*
> *and the disgrace of his people he will take away from*
> *all the earth,*
> *for the Lord has spoken (Is. 25:6, 8).*

The promise of bread, voluminous and appetising, prepared for a multitude, offers us a powerful image of God's infinite bounty towards the whole world. The Kingdom of God does not exist simply to decorate or embellish the table of Christians. The promise of the Kingdom is the offer of abundant life, life in all its fullness, to all peoples. Together as Christians, we are called *already* to express God's extraordinary promise, and to point, by how we live, to a peaceful, just world in which all humankind will eat together.

> [T]hey shall beat their swords into plowshares,
> and their spears into pruning hooks;
> nation shall not lift up sword against nation,
> neither shall they learn war any more (Is. 2:4b).

> All this is from God, who reconciled us to himself through Christ, and has given us the ministry of reconciliation (2 Cor. 5:18).

The Two Women at the Empty Tomb (Matt. 27:59–61; 28:1–10)

Even in my earliest childhood, I remember being moved by the story of the women at the empty tomb. One of the least 'hidden' of the stories of women in this Gospel, the passage is as majestic as it is powerful and miraculous. At the same time, I find it rich with immensely human detail, and never tire of reading it.

> *So Joseph took the body and wrapped it in a clean linen cloth and laid it in his own new tomb, which he had hewn in the rock. He then rolled a great stone to the door of the tomb and went away. Mary Magdalene and the other Mary were there, sitting opposite the tomb* (Matt. 27:59–61).

> *After the Sabbath, as the first day of the week was dawning, Mary Magdalene and the other Mary went to see the tomb. And suddenly there was a great earthquake; for an angel of the Lord, descending from heaven, came and rolled back the stone and sat on it. His appearance was like lightning, and his clothing white as snow. For fear of him the guards shook and became like dead men. But the angel said*

> to the women, "Do not be afraid; I know that you are looking for Jesus who was crucified. He is not here; for he has been raised, as he said. Come, see the place where he lay. Then go quickly and tell his disciples, 'He has been raised from the dead, and indeed he is going ahead of you to Galilee; there you will see him.' This is my message for you." So they left the tomb quickly with fear and great joy, and ran to tell his disciples. Suddenly Jesus met them and said, "Greetings!" And they came to him, took hold of his feet, and worshiped him. Then Jesus said to them, "Do not be afraid; go and tell my brothers to go to Galilee; there they will see me" (Matt. 28:1–10).

If we were to just gloss over the text without reading too carefully, we might summarise it in these terms,

> Grief at Jesus' death has glued these women to the tomb for several days, which is why they are still there when the angel of God rolls back the stone in front of the sepulchre. He gives them a message for the apostles. The women leave straight away. When they meet the risen Christ en route, he gives them the same message.

However, as we have found in our previous reflections, a more detailed reading, in search of the yeast of the Kingdom, encourages us, deepens our understanding and propels us into new ways of thinking and acting.

The Context of the Resurrection

Matthew tells us that two women are present at the burial of Jesus (Matt. 27:61): Mary Magdalene and 'the other' Mary at her side. The author is undoubtedly referring to Mary the mother of James and Joseph (Matt. 27:56). As these two women have also been present at the crucifixion and death of Jesus, they can testify that Jesus has not in any way escaped suffering and death. Paul expresses it in this way when he writes that Christ,

> *emptied himself,*
> *taking the form of a slave,*
> *being born in human likeness.*
> *And being found in human form,*
> *he humbled himself*
> *and became obedient to the point of death—*
> *even death on a cross (Phil. 2:7–8).*

At the beginning of Chapter 28, we come across these women again as they gaze at the sepulchre. They are witnesses once more to the reality of Jesus' death. Matthew offers no details of the lives of these two women, not even of the life of Mary Magdalene. Like the other women in the group, she must have followed and served Jesus since the beginning of his ministry in Galilee. The Gospel of Luke confirms that women indeed accompanied Jesus and the twelve,

> *The twelve were with him, as well as some women who had been cured of evil spirits and infirmities: Mary, called Magdalene, from whom seven demons had gone out ... (Luke 8:1b–2).*

Luke makes it clear: Mary Magdalene was a woman with a past not unlike many others. Hence, for her to have become a disciple, the moment of her healing must have been a very powerful one. It is striking that Mary Magdalene is not identified by any family ties, or by reference to any relationship as wife or mother. She is simply designated by the name of the place from which she came.

Magdala was a prosperous commercial centre in Galilee, with a diverse population. The town was well-known for the resistance offered to the Roman occupation by some of its inhabitants, and violence often erupted. The Romans imposed heavy taxes upon the Galilean population. At one point in the history of the region, members of the Roman military had arrested a number of men and forced them under torture to declare an income greater than it really was. The men were subsequently faced with a demand for a higher amount of tax than what would otherwise have been imposed, and those who refused to pay were put to death.[72] Mary of Magdalene may well have known this story. She was probably no stranger to violence and death.

While Magdala is filled with mistrust, Jesus offers a vision of a different reality: a world healed from its hatreds. He announces not the 'kingdom' of the Roman empire, but the reign of God. In Jesus' company, Mary of Magdala learns the power of forgiveness, the magnetism of love and the meaning of service. Once in Jerusalem, however, she finds herself once again confronted with the worst of human sinfulness as she witnesses the torture and death of Jesus.

Corrie and Betsie ten Boom (1892–1983 and 1885–1944)

Amongst the Christian women of recent times who have remained true to the Kingdom despite being confronted with the very worst of human sinfulness, it is hard to find a more moving testimony than that of Corrie ten Boom and her sister Betsie. These two women experienced

---

[72] Esther De Boer, trans. John Bowden, *Mary Magdalene* (London, UK: SCM, 1997), p. 26.

the power of Christ's resurrection in a place of death. While Corrie's autobiography in English is entitled *The Hiding Place*, the story of these sisters is in many ways anything but hidden. On the contrary, it is well-known internationally and has escaped the hiddenness of many of the other stories in this volume. Yet there are elements of Corrie's autobiography that have undoubtedly stayed in the shadows, and some of these shine an even greater light on the Kingdom values by which she, her sister and her father courageously lived. We shall endeavour to note them as this chapter proceeds.

Brought up in a large house in Haarlem, with a door as wide open as the hearts of the family who lived there, the two sisters had no idea of what the future might bring. From a Dutch reformed family, Corrie and Betsie lived with their father, a widowed watchmaker whose shop was on the ground floor of the house at street level. He would welcome with open arms everyone who arrived at their door asking for help. Convinced that no one should wait to live out their witness to the Kingdom, the ten Booms always managed to find an extra spoonful in the saucepan. In sharing a foretaste of the banquet of the Kingdom with those they gathered around their table, they had no inkling of what God had in store for them.

During the Second World War, the Nazi occupation brought hardships for all, but it was exceptionally terrible for Jewish members of the population. It had been hard from the very beginning, but became increasingly dangerous. A prayer was rising inside Corrie's heart, "Lord, Jesus, I offer myself for Your people. In any way. Any place. Any time."[73] This extraordinarily courageous

---

73   Ten Boom, *The Hiding Place*, 74.

prayer was to be answered when, one night in 1942, there was a knock at the door. A Jewish woman with a suitcase stood on the doorstep and simply said that she had been told that the ten Booms would be able to help her. Staying as true to the family's reputation for welcome as to the values of the Kingdom, the family invited her in. Two nights later, an elderly couple arrived with the same story. Very quickly the ten Boom household became a refuge—a 'hiding place'—for Jews and others in need. While the political situation grew horrifically worse around them, the life of the Kingdom continued to be celebrated in their home.

Corrie had to learn to live a double life very speedily. On the one hand, she needed to appear to be a model citizen in the eyes of the Nazi authorities. On the other hand, she was called to be a model citizen in the eyes of God, hiding Jews in danger, finding them safe places to move on to, and providing them with false papers necessary for both food and escape. The first Dutch woman to qualify as a watchmaker, Corrie assisted her father in the workshop and used her professional life as a cover for her clandestine activity. If someone from the resistance rang to ask her to repair a lady's watch, she understood that there was a Jewish woman who needed a hiding place. A request in relation to a very old gentleman's watch let her know that it was an elderly Jewish man who needed refuge.

The ten Booms had a small hiding place constructed in their house. It was at the back of a bedroom on the top floor, as far as possible from the front door, to allow the maximum amount of time for residents to reach it if ever there was a raid. After regular practices, the secret residents were able to get up the stairs and into the narrow hide-out within a matter of seconds. They became adept at leaving no tell-tale signs of their presence, which might give them away.

Just as the two Marys of our Bible passage refuse to flee, and stay with Jesus right to the tomb, Corrie and Betsie, together with their father, also took the brave decision to stay faithful to their work. The more severe the nature of the occupation became, the riskier their activities grew to be. A growing number of townspeople seemed to be aware of what was going on under their roof. One day their young apprentice was arrested by the Gestapo while he was on his way to warn one of the houses in the network that a search was coming. Corrie wrote later,

> Once again we considered stopping the work. Once again we discovered we could not. That night Father and Betsie and I prayed long after the others had gone to bed. We knew that in spite of daily mounting risks we had no choice but to move forward. This was evil's hour: we could not run away from it. Perhaps only when human effort had done its best and failed, would God's power alone be free to work.[74]

Corrie's fears proved to be justified shortly afterwards, when the Gestapo raided the house. Those who were hiding were not found, but Corrie, Betsie and their father were arrested. They were taken to the Gestapo headquarters in Holland. Seeing an old man standing in front of him, the officer in charge of the questioning wanted to send Corrie's father back home.

---

[74] Ten Boom, *The Hiding Place*, 118–119.

However, at the risk of his life, Corrie's father remained true to the Kingdom,

> "If I go home today," he said evenly and clearly, "tomorrow I will open my door again to any man in need who knocks."[75]

> These words led to his imprisonment, and Corrie and Betsie never saw their father again. Elderly and fragile, he died several days later.

Those who, like the ten Booms, stay faithful to the Kingdom are called to confront the false values of the kingdoms of the world. As we have seen through the witness of Alice Domon, our fidelity to the Kingdom does not hide us under a protective security blanket. Faith is not an insurance policy, and there is no deep-pile carpet for the pilgrim to walk on. Jesus never promises to spare us the hardships or the challenges that may meet us when we are obedient to God's authority. He only promises that those who are faithful to the Cross will know the power of his resurrection.

The Power of the Resurrection

Let us return to the story of the empty tomb. Ministers and scholars have often suggested that it is grief combined with an immobilising, heavy despair that pins the two Marys to the tomb. Perhaps, however, it is exactly the opposite. If Corrie continued to work believing that God would act even when human beings had done their very worst, the two Marys in Matthew's account could undoubtedly believe this too. They

---

75 Ten Boom, *The Hiding Place*, 131.

have followed Jesus on the way to Jerusalem, during which he has announced three times that he will rise again from the dead. Having stayed faithful to him to the cross, they are now eagerly anticipating the great event that he has promised. They may not know the form it will take. Nonetheless, in contrast to the twelve, who have run away believing that their world has fallen apart, these women continue to wait eagerly for the moment when the Kingdom will break through.

The news they have been expecting is announced in the very graveyard in which the body of Jesus has been buried. The place that offers the most sombre expression of death becomes the very context in which the joy of new life is proclaimed. In the mysterious ways of the Kingdom, the place of despair and desolation is precisely where the powerful new life of God is made known.

> **Corrie and Betsie ten Boom (cont'd)**
>
> Not unlike the two Marys, Corrie and her sister were also to become witnesses of Christ's resurrection life right inside a place of death: a Nazi concentration camp. The two sisters were first taken to Scheveningen prison, in Holland. There, Corrie spent four months in quarantine, recovering from illness. Imprisoned in darkness in a minute cell, she had time to reflect and pray. She was convinced that the Gospels offered a pattern for the action of God. As she re-read the Gospel stories, Corrie began to understand more of the great purposes of God,
>
>> Was it possible that this—all of this that seemed so wasteful and so needless—this war, Scheveningen prison, this very cell, none of it was unforeseen or accidental? Could it be part of the pattern first

revealed in the Gospels? Hadn't Jesus—and here my reading became intent indeed—hadn't Jesus been defeated as utterly and unarguably as our little group and our small plans had been?

But ... if the Gospels were truly the pattern of God's activity, then defeat was only the beginning. I would look around at the bare little cell and wonder what conceivable victory could come from a place like this.[76]

At this moment in time, Corrie had no idea that she would soon be a witness to the life of the Kingdom that would overflow in a place of death.

At Scheveningen, Corrie was re-united with her sister and, together, they were taken to Ravensbrück: the principal Nazi concentration camp for women in Germany. In the course of the war, 50,000 women died there. Betsie was one of them. Some died of un-treated illness, others of starvation, exhaustion or despair. Some were shot, or tortured then hanged or transferred to the gas chambers at Auschwitz. Others were subjected to medical experiments or amputations, which killed them or left them handicapped.

In Ravensbrück, the sisters were surrounded with fear and despair. Hatred and death were everywhere. But even as Betsie grew physically weaker every day, the yeast of the Kingdom was still powerfully at work in her. How should they live in such a place? Betsie received the answer to her immense question in the words of Scripture, "Comfort the frightened, help the weak, be patient with everyone. See that none of you repays evil

---

[76] Ten Boom, *The Hiding Place*, 142–143.

for evil, but always seek to do good to one another and to all ..."[77]

The two women wanted to live the great promise of the Kingdom in the context in which God had placed them. There was no time to lose. They decided to put the verse into practice. During the day, they survived in inhuman conditions, and at night they prayed with the women who wanted to join them. There were more and more of them, of different nationalities and from different Christian traditions,

> They were services like no others ... A single meeting might include a recital of the Magnificat in Latin by a group of Roman Catholics, a whispered hymn by some Lutherans, and a sotto-voce chant by Eastern Orthodox women. With each moment the crowd around us would swell ...

> At last either Betsie or I would open the Bible. Because only the Hollanders could understand the Dutch text we would translate aloud in German. And then we would hear the life-giving words passed back along the aisles in French, Polish, Russian, Czech, back into Dutch. They were little previews of heaven, these evenings beneath the light bulb. I would think of Haarlem, each substantial church set behind its wrought-iron fence and its barrier of doctrine. And I would know again that in darkness God's truth shines most clear.[78]

---

77   Ibid., 185.
78   Ibid., 188.

The feast of God's Kingdom without walls was already being celebrated in their dormitory. It became their place of worship and, thanks to the fleas that infested the place, the guards never crossed the threshold. Worship could continue uninterrupted. Prisoners confronted daily by hatred and violence were saved from descending into the same abyss and encouraged to remain respectful towards one another.

> I would look about us as Betsie read, watching the light leap from face to face. More than conquerors ... It was not a wish. It was a fact. We knew it, we experienced it minute by minute—poor, hated, hungry. We are more than conquerors. Not "we shall be." We are! Life in Ravensbrück took place on two separate levels, mutually impossible. One, the observable, external life, grew every day more horrible. The other, the life we lived with God, grew daily better, truth upon truth, glory upon glory.[79]

Betsie was convinced that the promise of the Kingdom extended not just to the prisoners and the countries they represented, but beyond them. The promise extended to all people, including those living in the thrall of Nazi ideology. During times of prayer with Corrie, Betsie insisted that they pray, too, for the guards. They needed to intercede for the healing of Germany as much as for the rest of Europe. As they prayed, the two women started to reflect on what they would do in years to come when the war was over. They dreamed of opening a large house where those wounded by life in the concentration camps could come and mend.

---

79   Ten Boom, *The Hiding Place*, 182.

> Then a short while before her death, Betsie shared with Corrie the vision she had received: that of creating a camp for healing in a former concentration camp. Those whose lives had been poisoned by an evil ideology based on hatred and violence would be welcomed and have an opportunity to learn the ways of love. Betsie had truly grasped that the greatness of the Kingdom is to be announced in the very place that has known the worst of human sinfulness.

The Proclamation of the Resurrection

Let us interrupt the powerful story of the ten Boom sisters and look again at the Easter story that Matthew tells. The anticipation of the two women at the tomb is rewarded: they are entrusted by the angel of God with an amazing message. They are to announce the great news of the resurrection to the apostles. On the way, they see Jesus with their own eyes and are able to testify that he is really risen. While the high priests and the elders circulate a rumour—a lie—to explain the disappearance of Jesus' body, these very women are in a position to affirm that the body of Christ has not been stolen by his disciples (Matt. 28:11–13).

Jesus entrusts to the women the same message that the angel of God has done, "go and tell my brothers to go to Galilee; there they will see me" (Matt. 28:10).

God's ways are not our ways! At the time of Jesus, a woman's word was not generally thought to be trustworthy. This situation was closely linked to her inferior social position. Because most women did not have the possibility of receiving an education, many believed that they did not have the intellectual capacity to be educated. It was claimed, therefore, that a woman had neither the wisdom nor the competence to speak.

In addition, the image of the ideal woman at the time was one of a woman who did not raise her voice to those in authority over her. This silence was considered to be the perfect expression not only of a woman's inferior social standing but also of her submission and obedience to her father or her husband, and consequently to God. The vast majority of moral philosophers of the time were in agreement on this point of woman's submission, even if they presented different arguments to account for their point of view.

It is already remarkable that Jesus, breaking from the usual practices of his time, has women amongst his companions and encourages their presence during his ministry. It is even more remarkable that the angel of God entrusts to the women the proclamation of the Gospel: Jesus is risen! If today we confess Jesus Christ crucified and risen, it is in part thanks to the fidelity of the women present at the cross and the empty tomb. They act in obedience to Jesus, rather than conform to the silent stereotype of their time.

The seventeenth-century English Quaker, Margaret Fell,[80] indignant and frustrated at not being allowed to preach, found the example of the women at the tomb to be an inspiration. She drew on their testimony in her pamphlet 'Women's Speaking Justified',

> Thus we see that Jesus owned the Love and Grace that appeared in Women, and did not despise it: and by what is recorded in the Scriptures, he received as much Love, Kindness, Compassion, and tender Dealing towards him from Women, as he did from any others, both in his Life time, and

---

80   (1614–1702) English Quaker, wife of George Fox, imprisoned for her faith.

also after they had exercised their Cruelty upon him ...

Mark this, ye despisers of the Weakness of Women, and look upon your selves to be so wise: But Christ Jesus doth not so; for he makes use of the weak: For when he met the Women after he was risen, he said unto them, *All Hail!* And they came and held him by the Feet, and worshipped him; then said Jesus unto them, *Be not afraid, go tell my Brethren that they go into Galilee* ...

Mark this, you that despise and oppose the Message of the Lord God that he sends by Women; What had become of the Redemption of the whole Body of Mankind, if they had not cause to believe the Message that the Lord Jesus sent by these Women, of and concerning his Resurrection?[81]

The tone of Margaret Fell's writing echoes the same sense of urgency and need to communicate that we find in the Biblical passage itself. I am always struck by the vitality of the message of Christ's resurrection, and the need to make the news known without delay! The story has great intensity. The message is so big, so explosive, so devastating, there is not a second to lose. The angel of God says to the women, "Then **go quickly** and tell his disciples, 'He has been raised from the dead, and indeed he is going ahead of you to Galilee'" (Matt. 28:7).

The women show little willingness to disobey him. On the contrary, we rather have the impression that they cannot run quickly enough. The Good News grasps the women to

---

81   Margaret Fell, *Women's Speaking Justified, Proved and Allowed of by the Scriptures*, published 1666.

their very core and they simply cannot contain themselves, "So they left the tomb **quickly** with fear and great joy, and **ran** to tell his disciples" (Matt. 28:8).

The news is so great and so urgent that it propels them physically forward. These are not silent, submissive women lurking demurely in a corner smiling through their tears, but dynamic and passionate communicators of the Gospel, rushing to share the message in obedience to Christ.

Margaret Fell, like countless others, was also passionately aware of the greatness of the message that she needed to share. Betsie ten Boom also. The day before she died, she whispered to her sister,

> ... must tell people what we have learned here. We must tell them that there is no pit so deep that He is not deeper still. They will listen to us, Corrie, because we have been here.[82]

Betsie had the wisdom to see that true testimony needed to be built on true experience. It seems to me very often that in offering our testimony to others, whether in speech or in song—person to person, or in a service—we can fall into the habit of simply reiterating well-tried and tested phrases that are well-known in our churches. Here I am not referring to the great Creeds, but to the spiritual language that sometimes goes out of fashion as quickly as it came in. Often we can feel that our testimony must correspond to the ways in which other people in our fellowship have expressed theirs, and we fear being judged if our own language does not conform. But the risen Christ tells us not to fear. Like the two Marys at the empty tomb, like Corrie and Betsie, we only need to be authentic. It is a question of speaking of our true experience of God, without pride and without shame, and of not being

---

82   Ten Boom, *The Hiding Place*, 202.

frightened of raising the beautiful voices that God has given us. We have no need to hold back. The Good News is too big for us to keep quiet.

Made Bold by the Resurrection

In Matthew's Gospel, we read the words of the angel, "Do not be afraid!" This is not the first time in the Gospel that this message has been announced. When Mary the mother of Jesus becomes pregnant, the angel of God who appears to Joseph tells him not to be afraid (Matt. 1:20). It is the word that Jesus speaks to the twelve when he warns them of persecutions to come (Matt. 10:26), and when he walks on the water towards his disciples (Matt. 14:27). God knows us well, fearful as we are in so many different ways. And he never stops reminding us that ultimately, held in his love, we have nothing to fear.

It is the same message at the empty tomb, spoken by the risen Christ. The resurrection changes everything, so no wonder we are shaking at the prospect. Yet we have nothing to be afraid of, as Paul reminds us,

> *Who is to condemn? It is Christ Jesus, who died, yes, who was raised, who is at the right hand of God, who indeed intercedes for us. Who will separate us from the love of Christ? Will hardship, or distress, or persecution, or famine, or nakedness, or peril, or sword? [...] No, in all these things we are more than conquerors through him who loved us. For I am convinced that neither death, nor life, nor angels, nor rulers, nor things present, nor things to come, nor powers, nor height, nor depth, nor anything else in all creation, will be able to separate us from the love of God in Christ Jesus our Lord (Rom. 8:34–35; 37–39).*

In contrast to the followers of Jesus who receive this great message from God with joy, Matthew shows how others in the Gospel story are controlled and painfully diminished by their fears. Matthew describes Herod's reaction, for example, on receiving the news of Jesus' birth. A collaborator with the Romans, he is alarmed to learn from the wise men that they are searching for the King of the Jews, "When King Herod heard this, **he was frightened**" (Matt. 2:3). The knowledge that Herod, the one in power, is fearful then breeds fear right across the general population, "and all Jerusalem with him" (Matt. 2:3).

Later in the Gospel, Matthew tells us how Herod the tetrarch wants the death of John the Baptist, who has denounced his marriage to his brother's wife, "Though Herod wanted to put him to death, **he feared the crowd**, because they regarded him as a prophet" (Matt. 14:5).

Pilate is also motivated by fear. Matthew recounts how Pilate would like to spare Jesus from crucifixion. He is nonetheless responsible to his superiors for maintaining order in his territory and he fears the anger of the crowd,

> So when Pilate saw that he could do nothing, but rather that ***a riot was beginning***, he took some water and washed his hands before the crowd, saying, "I am innocent of this man's blood; see to it yourselves" (Matt. 27:24).

The Jewish authorities also live in fear of the crowd at the time when they interrogate Jesus about the nature of his authority. These men find themselves in a very tight situation when Jesus turns their question around and asks about the nature of John's authority,

> *Did the baptism of John come from heaven, or was it of*

human origin?" And they argued with one another, "If we say, 'From heaven,' he will say to us, 'Why then did you not believe him?' But if we say, 'Of human origin,' **we are afraid of the crowd***; for all regard John as a prophet" (Matt. 21:25–26).*

These same authorities fear losing their own authority over the people. When these men want to get rid of Jesus, they are once again held back by their fears,

They wanted to arrest him, but ***they feared the crowds****, because they regarded him as a prophet (Matt. 21:46).*

Everyone is frightened of losing power and authority, and of being controlled by others rather than being in control. The two kings, the governor who represents the Roman empire, and the Jewish authorities all act to preserve their power and glory.

Matthew reveals that this fear is intimately linked with acts of violence. At the time of Jesus' birth, Herod massacres the children of his own people (Matt. 2:16), while Herod the tetrarch finally has John the Baptist executed (Matt. 14:10). Pilate delivers up Jesus to the crowd (Matt. 27:26). Meanwhile the Jewish authorities have Jesus arrested and condemned to death at an illegal trial. Fear of losing control can open the door to all that leads to death. We do not have to look very far in the events of the world today to see how much this same fear is still at the root of violence, oppression and murder.

While human authority is founded on the uncertainty and vicissitudes of human power, Jesus' authority comes from God. The resurrection of Christ confirms the sovereignty of God and the eternal values of the Kingdom. Those who serve him have nothing to fear; they have only to trust,

> *Through him you have come to trust in God, who raised him from the dead and gave him glory, so that your faith and hope are set on God (1 Peter 1:21).*

Our fear is dispelled when we place all our confidence in the life of God made known in Christ. The apostle Paul reminds Timothy of the same message, though in different words. Timothy can be proud of the Gospel and of all those who, like Paul, are imprisoned for having witnessed to the Kingdom,

> *for God did not give us a spirit of cowardice, but rather a spirit of power and of love and of self-discipline. Do not be ashamed, then, of the testimony about our Lord or of me his prisoner, but join with me in suffering for the gospel, relying on the power of God (2 Tim. 1:7–8).*

Corrie and Betsie ten Boom (cont'd)

Let us pick up the threads of Corrie's story once again and see it in the light of what we have just read in the Gospel story. Like the two Marys, Corrie was unashamed of the Gospel, and the boldness with which she dared to speak to one of her captors is nothing short of remarkable. In her autobiography, she recounts the interrogation she underwent at Scheveningen, before being transferred to Ravensbrück. She found herself facing questioning in the office of a lieutenant of the Nazi administration, who began by asking her about a particular operation carried out by the resistance. Ascertaining that Corrie knew nothing about it, he started to question her about her other activities. Not wanting to endanger the lives of those with whom she had been working before her arrest, Corrie had the presence of mind to talk about a different 'other activity': that of working with people with learning difficulties. When the lieutenant expressed huge surprise that she should be seeking the conversion of "half-wits" instead of those of sound mind, Corrie replied with the confidence of the women at the empty tomb,

> "The truth, Sir," I said, swallowing, "is that God's view-point is sometimes different from ours ... In the Bible I learn that God values us not for our strength or our brains but simply because He has made us. Who knows, in His eyes a half-wit may be worth more than a watchmaker. Or—a lieutenant."[83]

The lieutenant immediately dismissed her and Corrie was left wondering if she had said too much. The following day, she was called back and she expected to be questioned further about her clandestine activity. However, the lieutenant talked to her about his own anxieties and his fear for his children. She describes his extraordinary honesty, as he admitted that he hated the work he had been assigned to in the prison,

> Miss ten Boom, it is possible that I appear to you a powerful person. I wear a uniform, I have a certain authority over those under me. But I am in prison, dear lady from Haarlem, a prison stronger than this one.[84]

---

83 Ten Boom, *The Hiding Place*, 151
84 Ibid., 153.

Beneath the symbols of glory and human authority, the lieutenant, like the authorities described so vividly in Matthew's Gospel, was living in fear. Corrie, on the other hand, was sustained by a faith that gave her both the confidence to be true to the Kingdom and also the courage to speak. Corrie's account of this extraordinary conversation presents a stark and dramatic contrast between the life that is lived in fear and the one that is lived in faith. Corrie is in no doubt as to which life knows the greater freedom, and she leaves to the reader the opportunity to make the choice.

As Christians today, we are often scared of giving expression to our faith, or puzzled as to how to do so in a way that is meaningful to others. While some Christians in certain parts of the world face persecution on many levels, for others it is not a question of risking our lives in order to witness to our faith, but of being misunderstood, side-lined and thought to be strange, if not deranged. On occasions, it may mean defying the law. The secularism by which many of us are surrounded, to say nothing of the forceful expressions of atheism, can hold us back and make us fear to speak truly and honestly as ourselves, as the people of faith we are called to be.

What is more, without our desiring to be, we are the representatives of a Church whose past sins are only too well-known or well-rehearsed: the crusades and the wars of religion, the alignment of the Church with oppressive powers that have stripped the poor of their wealth, the Church's subjugation of women, her collusion with racism and her silence in relation to paedophile crimes. Yet without our renewed and truthful witness to the values of the Kingdom, the suspicions and justified condemnations expressed by the many will linger on. We live in challenging times for people of faith. There is no doubt that the need for all of us to live and breathe the true values of the Gospel with courage has become an urgent priority.

No need to pronounce a theological treaty every time we open our mouth, or to repeat without sensitivity the kinds of phrases we may hear in church. We are called to give an account of the faith that is *within* us. Speaking with integrity and honesty, we can be rightly proud of the Gospel, and of the God who has called us to follow Christ. Above all others, it is our Christian identity that shapes and moulds us, just as powerfully as the yeast of the Kingdom works within us.

> *When they hand you over, do not worry about how you are to speak or what you are to say; for what you are to say will be given to you at that time; for it is not you who speak, but the Spirit of your Father speaking through you (Matt. 10:19–20).*

The Feast Prepared for all People

It is very striking that in Matthew's story of the empty tomb, Jesus refers to the apostles as "his brothers". Elsewhere in this Gospel, Jesus very rarely uses this word for describing the twelve. However, in Chapter 12 we read,

> *And pointing to his disciples, he said, "Here are my mother and my brothers! For whoever does the will of my Father in heaven is my brother and sister and mother" (Matt. 12:49–50).*

At this point in his ministry, Jesus defines his true brothers and sisters and mothers as those who are obedient to God. But at the empty tomb, Jesus describes as brothers those who have not been obedient, and who, in deserting him, have done the exact opposite of taking up their cross and following him. Yet by still calling them 'brothers', Jesus heralds the new community, built upon his death and resurrection, of which he has become "the firstborn within a large family" (Rom. 8:29).

> *For you did not receive a spirit of slavery to fall back into fear, but you have received a spirit of adoption. When we cry, "Abba! Father!" it is that very Spirit bearing witness with our spirit that we are children of God (Rom. 8:15–6).*

So, by entrusting them with his message to his "brothers", Jesus invites these women to bring a message of forgiveness. These men have betrayed, denied and deserted him, but they still belong to him. Matthew is not interested in whether these women are angry or disappointed by the behaviour of the twelve, or whether they think they deserve punishment. He is only interested in recounting how Jesus commands those who have indeed been faithful to go to those who have not been, and announce the news of his resurrection and forgiveness. In entrusting this message for his 'brothers', Jesus gives expression to the great Good News at the heart of the Kingdom,

> *since all have sinned and fall short of the glory of God; they are now justified by his grace as a gift, through the redemption that is in Christ Jesus (Rom. 3:23–24).*

In their obedience to the risen Jesus, these women become the first bearers of the amazing message of reconciliation accomplished by the death and resurrection of Christ. This Good News has power to heal the greatest hurts and divisions. As the letter to the Ephesians explains,

> *He has abolished the law with its commandments and ordinances, that he might create in himself one new*

humanity in place of the two, thus making peace, and might reconcile both groups to God in one body through the cross, thus putting to death that hostility through it. So he came and proclaimed peace to you who were far off and peace to those who were near (Eph. 2:15–17).

Corrie and Betsie ten Boom (cont'd)

Corrie was also aware that the Gospel had power to heal. The hurts and divisions to which she was a witness were amongst the very worst known to Europe in modern times. After the war, she exercised an important international ministry in which the vision that Betsie had shared before her death became a reality. Corrie created a centre in a large house in Bloemendaal in the Netherlands and transformed a former concentration camp into a place of welcome. Invited throughout the world to speak of her experiences of Ravensbrück, Corrie shared her testimony and that of her sister.

Corrie was particularly conscious of the need for her message to be heard in Germany. In her autobiography, she recounts how every time she crossed the frontier, she was aware of entering a land in which both cities and human hearts had been reduced to ashes. In general, during her visits, she encountered people she had never met before. However, one Sunday, at the end of a service in a church in Munich at which she had been speaking, she recognised someone. This man had been a guard at Ravensbrück, and had been in charge of the bathroom. He had treated Betsie with untold cruelty when she was ill and frail. Corrie describes how setting eyes on this man brought everything back to her: the pile of clothes that the women had been ordered to take off, the room full of soldiers mocking the women's nudity, and her sister's frail condition.

This man came up to Corrie and thanked her profusely for the message she had shared with the congregation, which had reminded him of God's forgiveness for his sins. Corrie tells how the man wanted to shake her hand, but that she remained frozen and unable to move. However, beneath her anger, she nonetheless knew that Jesus Christ has died for this man too. She recounts how first she prayed, asking Christ to help her forgive the man. She then attempted to extend her hand, but was unable to do so. At that point she prayed differently, "Jesus, I cannot forgive him. Give me Your forgiveness." She tried to extend her hand again,

> As I took his hand, the most incredible thing happened. From my shoulder along my arm and through my hand a current seemed to pass from me to him, while into my heart sprang a love for this stranger that almost overwhelmed me.
>
> And so I discovered that it is not on our forgiveness any more than on our goodness that the world's healing depends, but on His.[85]

Corrie offers a simple account of profound spiritual truth, expressed in and through her in a physical way. Her description of what happened echoes something of the physicality expressed by the two Marys, running from the empty tomb to share the news of the resurrection with Jesus' "brothers". It also sends us back to our reading of the woman with the

---

85   Ten Boom, *The Hiding Place*, 220–221.

flow of blood (Chapter IV), who extends her hand to touch Jesus' garment, in courageous faith and daring anticipation of what God is going to do. Those who witness to the Kingdom are called to prophetic, imaginative and daring action, in the firm trust that God recognises such faith and comes to meet and affirm it. Just like Corrie ten Boom, like the women at the empty tomb, each one of us is called to witness in this way. The feast is prepared for all people and all are invited to eat side by side.

Our reading of this beautiful and inspiring passage has revealed the faith, courage and fidelity of the women at the empty tomb. The risen Christ entrusts them with the good news of the resurrection and commands them to announce the forgiveness that he is offering to those who abandoned him. More than that: these women leave the tomb running in order to broadcast the news with urgency. The message is so big that the women are unable to keep it for themselves. The haste expressed by these women reminds us that the Good News is not something to share on a day when we have nothing else to do. It demands an immediate response. No point waiting for the day we know the Bible better, or have developed a more profound spirituality, or reached a maturity in faith or an easier work situation. With the yeast active within us, the Gospel is to be lived today, and the more challenging our context, the more faithful we need to be. The God who has reconciled us to him is the one who entrusts to us the ministry of reconciliation, and who gives us the confidence to know that nothing can extinguish in us the vision of the great feast, prepared for all humankind.

It is the appearance of the risen Christ that interrupts the women in their haste. Seeing him, they grasp his feet and prostrate themselves. This is a beautiful moment of worship that confirms the sovereignty of Christ and the call of the women. Matthew reminds us that through worship, we become more faithful as witnesses to the resurrection of Christ and the life of the Kingdom. Through worship, God renews our hope and strengthens us in faith. He reminds us of our call to witness. Then he sends us out on the road to serve him, by grace offering us the courage to speak and act.

When they nailed Jesus to the cross, the authorities of the kingdoms of this world imagined that they would put an end to both his teaching and to the hope of the Kingdom of God. The values of the Kingdom threatened and disturbed their own kingdoms. By witnessing to the empty tomb, by breaking with social convention in order to do so, the women are the first to understand that nothing can stand in the way of the dynamism of the reign of God or diminish the grandeur of its promise. Thanks to the women's courageous faithfulness, the Good News of the Gospel is ripe to be proclaimed by us today.

Ah! Let us forgive as we ourselves have been forgiven! Let us love as we also have been loved! May the mind of Jesus Christ be in us.
Madeleine Blocher-Saillens[86]

Lord, I heartily desire of Thee, that Thou wilt of Thy merciful goodness forgive them that violence which they do, and have done unto me. So be it, Lord.
Anne Askew[87]

---

86   (1881–1971), Baptist theologian, first French woman minister, appointed in 1929. Blocher-Saillens, *Les Sept Paroles de la Croix*, p. 26.
87   (1551–1546), English, protestant martyr.

The Yeast in Our Lives: Ambassadors of the Kingdom Today

Christ has no body but yours,
No hands, no feet on earth but yours,
Yours are the eyes with which he looks compassion on this world,
Yours are the feet with which he walks to do good,
Yours are the hands, with which he blesses all the world.
Attributed to Teresa of Avila[88]

God, here's my Bible, here's my money, here's me. Use me, God.
Gladys Aylward[89]

Although I am still very naïve in many ways,
And ignorant as well,
Yet God has nonetheless used my feeble witness
To bless his people.
Dora Yu[90]

How does God shape women to change the world around them? This is the question we have been reflecting on in the course of this book. To help us approach the question, we have been looking at Jesus' parable of the yeast and, in the light of

---

88   (1551–1582), Spanish religious, reformer, writer and mystic.
89   (1902–1970), English missionary in China.
90   (1873–1931), Chinese physician, evangelist and missionary in Korea and China, preacher, school and church planter. Her ministry saw the conversion of Watchman Nee.

it, reading stories not only of women in Matthew's Gospel, but also of more modern women, their counterparts in witness. We have looked at their faithfulness and their courage, their unshakeable determination and their feisty witness. It has been both a surprising and an inspiring study that has taken us on a wide-ranging journey into the rich and startling imagery of the parable.

The women whose stories we have reflected on may have come from a variety of times and places, but the yeast of the Kingdom was decidedly at work in each one of them. Daring to cross social boundaries and burst through the walls of cultural divides, these women have been witnesses first of all to the *inclusive* nature of the Kingdom. Their acts of adventurous faith have witnessed to the Kingdom that welcomes all. So, for example, we have watched in amazement as the woman with the flow of blood, seeking healing, has reached out and touched Jesus. We have been bowled over by the courage of the Gentile woman who has dared to come asking Jesus to heal her daughter. We have been inspired as Sojourner Truth, a freed black slave woman, overcame the boundaries of race and education to become an evangelist and abolitionist campaigner among white audiences. And we have smiled and wept at the struggles of Amy Carmichael, as she has rescued vulnerable children and offered a loving home to those at the farthest and most forgotten edges of the world's dough.

> **The yeast also reminded us of the loving, serving, sacrificial nature of the Kingdom that transforms us.**

Describing the action of the woman who took "and hid" yeast, the parable has also invited us to think about the hidden activity of the yeast. This has been a difficult theme for us to approach, given that the moment we talk of what is hidden, it immediately ceases to be so. Yet the women we have followed in this book are also witnesses to the *hidden nature* of the Kingdom. We looked at the names listed in Matthew's genealogy, noticing how the lives of women that might be judged scandalous from a superficial point of view, each offer glimpses of the Kingdom values that, later in the Gospel, Jesus himself will make known. We learned of the hidden Kingdom rising up in the heart of the woman with the flow of blood, as she decides to act in a way society would deem unacceptable. We saw how the woman with the perfume anoints Jesus' head and how the meaning of her action is hidden from those who criticise her. We noticed how the Kingdom was already at work in the hiddenness of Sojourner Truth's prayers as a slave, behind the walls of Death Row in which Karla Faye Tucker was incarcerated, and in the home Amy made for abandoned children, which remained hidden for many years because so many continued to deny the existence of the horrific reality she described. Through the testimony of Corrie ten Boom, we saw how the hidden Kingdom was active and powerful even in the heart of a concentration camp.

The yeast also reminded us of the loving, serving, *sacrificial nature* of the Kingdom that transforms us. We encountered the women whose faithful service to Jesus takes them all the way to the Cross. There, they grasp the true, humble nature of Jesus' kingship, which dramatically contrasts Herod's murderous nature. We watched the woman pouring expensive perfume over Jesus' head, in contrast to Judas who, in the next episode, gives Jesus up for his own financial gain. We were inspired by the servant hearts of Sabina Bell and Dorcas Price, working to bring welcome to some of the most forgotten people in society. We were moved by the faithfulness to Christ of Perpetua and Felicitas, Alice Domon and Betsie ten Boom, who gave their very lives to testify to the hope and vision of the Kingdom that was alive within them.

The parable has also reminded us that the Kingdom of God is *enduring and future-orientated*. It takes its time, and those who serve Christ are called to be faithful and persevering, as God is enduringly faithful to us. We have been stunned by the vision of the Canaanite woman who points to the future welcome of Gentiles into the Church. We have been surprised by the prophetic understanding of the woman who anoints Jesus with perfume. Amongst the modern testimonies, we have been heartened by Sojourner's call as a black woman to minister to white people, in promise of the reconciliation to come. We have also been moved to tears by the vision of Betsie ten Boom, sharing, even with her last breath, her dream of creating a healing centre to welcome those damaged by an ideology of hatred.

What might these women have to teach the Church about the call to serve in our own times? How can their witness serve as an encouragement to ours? As those who, in order to fulfil their calling, often needed to break with the conventions or traditions of their time, they have the power to speak to us out of their own contexts and into ours. They can offer us ways forward and urge us to be bold. For us to be faithful in our generation, we need to hear how they were faithful in theirs.

They Came Out of Hiding

Belonging to societies in which virtuous women were thought, to one degree or another, to belong to the private sphere, these women dared to step out into the big wide world. It is really striking that out of the Biblical women we have considered here, all but Peter's mother-in-law are to be found outside of their home. Peter's mother-in-law, certainly, is sick and confined to the house, and, when healed, serves Jesus in a domestic setting. Yet the others are all found outside of their private sphere. The woman with a flow of blood is out of doors, approaching Jesus in a crowd, while the Canaanite woman emerges out of the shadows to meet Jesus on the road. The woman who anoints Jesus' head has come out of her own home into the house of a leper in order to offer her prophetic action. Meanwhile, the women present at the cross have left home and family in rural Galilee to travel across country. They have followed Jesus up mountains, down roads and along beaches. The last time we catch sight of them they are still outside, in a graveyard, refusing to hide away, and then we see them rushing off to tell others the Good News. In a culture that preferred to keep women hidden, these Biblical women dare to be completely visible. They come out of the wings onto the stage and engage with Jesus in public.

The more modern Christian women we have looked at are also 'out there', witnessing to the Kingdom through all the social and political complexity of their times. So we have been enthralled by the story of Alice Domon, sharing the lives of the poorest and most oppressed people in Argentina. We have accompanied Sabina Bell as she has been schooled in the local church to become a servant of Christ outside of it, ministering to some of the most disadvantaged people. We have journeyed with Sojourner Truth as she left her slave's life behind her to become an itinerant preacher.

Through the powerful imagery of the yeast at work in the whole dough, the parable invites us to question our own boundaries. It challenges us to examine the ways in which we often seek to confine the activity of God, especially if we look for evidence of the Kingdom only in our churches or within the walls of our private and relational lives. The parable calls us to emerge from the comfortable bubbles in which we so often take refuge and seek for the Kingdom outside of them. It compels us to recognise that we can be a witness for Christ in all the contexts of our lives, both public and private. Whether at work, at leisure, at worship or at rest, Christ calls women to be visible, living the values of the Kingdom in every walk of life.

They Unashamedly Offered Their Gifts

The women we meet in this book, from different times and cultures, are faced with very different challenges. The testimony of each one of them is shaped and characterised by the particular gifts that they have been given. While we are not in a position to know what all the gifts of the Biblical women were, we have no difficulty working out that the woman with the flow of blood had the gift of nothing-to-lose daring, while the Canaanite woman was blessed with a quick wit, knife-like intelligence and a defiant spirit. Some of the women who followed Jesus were in a position to support him financially and the woman who anointed his head had the means to provide costly perfume. Peter's mother-in-law was gifted perhaps as a cook. As for the two Marys at the empty tomb, it may well be that they were unaware that they had a gift for speaking. But thanks to the commands of the angel and of Jesus, they were soon going to discover that they had a talent for proclaiming the Good News!

The former slave, Sojourner Truth, was a powerful public speaker and God used her in the way she courageously addressed crowds of people. She was gifted with a strong sense of humour, constantly put to the test in her moments of repartee with the crowds. Corrie ten Boom had other skills. Gifted in hospitality, she witnessed to the Kingdom by welcoming into her home those in danger of their lives. Amy Carmichael was gifted with leadership and entrepreneurial skills, to say nothing of her talent for writing. Meanwhile Alice Domon, with her strong relational abilities, had a great capacity for love for her fellow men and women, which equipped her to accompany and support those fighting for justice.

These women encourage us to believe that each one of us is called to be an ambassador of the Kingdom according to the unique talents with which God has entrusted us. The yeast is at work within each one of us. Women are not called to embrace false modesty, for fear of being thought to push themselves out in front of men, nor are they to protest they have nothing to offer, believing their role is demurely to hang back. On the contrary, if we believe that the yeast of the Kingdom is indeed at work within us, then we have no reason not to make the talents we have been given plainly visible, offering them into the mix. Whether we be gifted in management or music, accountancy or crafting, science or sport, our talents have a place in the Kingdom. In the great goodness and generosity of God, we are likely to discover other gifts we never knew we had, just waiting to be put to use. The yeast is constantly active and the dough of our lives does not stop growing.

They Took the Initiative

Rather than sitting waiting to be told what to do, these women take extraordinary initiatives. This is true first of all of the Biblical women. This is absolutely startling. We might have expected women at the time of Jesus to have been presented as retiring, modest and submissive figures. As we have already said earlier, the family house was organised very differently in the ancient world to the way it is usually organised today. A woman, whether an unmarried daughter, a married woman or a widow, was dependent on the father of the household or male relative, and her virtue would traditionally have been expressed through her submissive obedience to him.

However, the women we have seen in the Gospel are a long way from demonstrating any kind of reticence. The woman with a flow of blood devises a plan on her own before going out to Jesus, and does not even wait modestly to be addressed by him before reaching out and touching him. Meanwhile the Canaanite woman, far from being a polite, shrinking violet, is quite determined that Jesus' ministry extends to her and nothing will convince her otherwise. The woman who anoints Jesus' head does not appear to ask anyone's permission to do so, while the women who accompany Jesus from Galilee to Jerusalem defy the conventions of their day by leaving home. These women are not meek, unassuming and mild. On the contrary, they are passionate and dynamic, forging ahead and unafraid of putting their faith into practice.

The same might be said of the modern testimonies we have considered. They also break from the well-tried paths of witness taken by others of their time. At her husband's side, Sabina Bell moved from service in the church as the wife of a minister, to service alongside her husband as a social worker. Instead of working with the children of the upper-classes as many of her colleagues did, Amy Carmichael stepped out of line and worked with abused and forgotten children. Alice Domon, along with other religious, eventually resigned from her order, believing in so doing that she might better share the lives of those she served. All of these women were people of their time, yes, and shaped by the societies in which they lived. Yet, each was willing when necessary to be unconventional in order to take initiatives for the Kingdom.

They encourage us to remember that women today are called to be ambassadors of the Kingdom, just as we are. God does not require us to adhere to ideals of 'truly feminine' qualities that tradition may have heaped upon us. We are not obliged to fulfil without question the expectations of parents or grandparents, or to conform to images of perfect Christian womanhood still often espoused by many of our churches. We are called only to follow Christ as ambassadors of the Kingdom in all aspects of our daily lives. That very call may well lead us to outgrow former ways of thinking and acting, and even to denounce them. That call will bring us to places where we discover new ways of responding fully to Christ's invitation and grow into the full human beings we are invited to become.

They Spoke Out

As we have mentioned before, in the ancient world, the virtuous woman was thought to be silent. A 'good' woman was to wait to be addressed by others. Yet Matthew is unafraid to recount the stories of women who raise their voices. The Canaanite woman just will not be quiet and, far from being reduced to silence, becomes more vocal. Pilate's wife, filled with the wisdom she has received, advises her husband what to do—and her judgement is accurate. Meanwhile, the women present at the empty tomb are actually commanded by both the angel and Jesus to go forth and tell. They are entrusted with the news of the resurrection and leave the tomb fired up with the message bursting out of them.

> The women we have looked at ... have shown us that ... discipleship is about daring to be truly faithful to Christ in all the contexts in which we live.

The same is true of the modern women we have considered. Far from being demure, these women were bold and ready to say what was what. Amy Carmichael was determined to tell the truth about children forced into prostitution, even if it was not the sort of thing 'successful' missionaries were meant to say. Alice Domon gave her very life for breaking the silence about the disappeared. Sojourner Truth was quick-witted and brave and in the face of vehement opposition, engaged in repartee with members of her audiences. She gradually gathered more and more courage in speaking, until she was strong and bold enough to share her own story and speak about the way in which as a slave she had been the victim of abuse and violence.

Women today are also called to speak out in a context in which we have the advantages of many different forms of communication. Not all may be talented as public orators or equipped with natural eloquence, and some may be in places of danger where speaking up and out is extremely costly. Depending on context, speaking out may require different degrees of courage, and for some, breaking the silence will demand huge spiritual strength. Yet we all have voices worthy of being heard, with an important message to share. The more women break with their silent past and demand to be heard, the more they will take their rightful place amongst the crowd of witnesses, men and women alike, called to give testimony to the yeast at work in the dough of all the world.

They Were Changed by Christ

The women we have encountered from Matthew's Gospel were all changed, whether they expected to be or not. The woman with the flow of blood and the Canaanite woman both had faith that their lives would be transformed by Jesus. Their trust was rewarded when their lives were changed in ways they hoped and expected. The lives of others of the women were transformed in ways that perhaps they did not expect. The mother of James and John started out hoping for an upwardly mobile change in circumstances but ended up following the crucified one to the cross. The other women who followed also may well have been surprised, not to say frightened, to see where they ended up. Yet their very presence at the cross is witness to their willingness to stay true and follow Jesus wherever he might lead.

The other modern women included in this book also all underwent profound transformation. Sabina started out as a minister's wife in the local church and ended up working with people with special needs. Sojourner Truth went from being a slave, to being a paid domestic help, to being an evangelist and abolitionist. Amy Carmichael started off as a traditional missionary and ended up fighting for laws that would prohibit child prostitution. Alice Domon grew increasingly committed to serving the people to whom she had been called and finally lost her life alongside them.

These women did not defy convention in order to be thought 'difficult' or 'overbearing'. If they broke with the traditional ideas of 'feminine' perfection, it was because they followed Christ, nothing less, nothing more. As they journeyed with Christ, obedient to him above all others, they recognised that the authority of the Kingdom is far above that of human empires, traditions and social norms. Following Christ led them to step out and speak out. Following Christ led them to offer their gifts willingly and unashamedly. Following Christ led them to be transformed in his image and they could not ever be the same again.

The women we have looked at have all pointed in these directions. They have shown us that for *both* women and men, discipleship is about daring to be truly faithful to Christ in all the contexts in which we live—the public sphere included. It is a call to overturn the boundaries, and leave behind the nets that have kept us preoccupied and the boats we expected to be rowing all our lives. It is the invitation to undertake an adventure through an encounter with Christ that transforms and energises. Every day lived as his disciple is a stepping out, and every day brings new surprises, discoveries and lessons in its wake. The more fiercely or unquestioningly the empires of this world seek to impose their false values upon us, the more faithful we need to be to the life of God's Kingdom.

I believe that if we are to hold true to the vision of God's Kingdom, we need to reflect more often on the parables of the Kingdom, daring to expose our hearts and minds to the images into which they invite us. They offer a myriad of possibilities, a kaleidoscope of pictures that can be as transformative of our lives as their meanings can be challenging. They open us up, rather than close us down, direct us to the future, and instead of giving us easy categories through which to see God, invite us to wait for insight and wisdom. The parable of the yeast has played its own amazing part in opening God's Kingdom up to us.

Those who have gone before us in the faith are now passing the baton on. Christ invites each one of us to open our hearts to the yeast of the Kingdom, and to live faithful to his call. The challenges are not at all the same as they were for our sisters in times past. It is for us, now, to explore ways to communicate the truth of the Gospel effectively for today. Coming as we do from a variety of Christian traditions, we all need the spiritual treasures of one another in order better to understand the length, breadth, height and depth of the love of Christ. Christ who invites us to follow him is always the same and the promise of the Kingdom has not changed. The yeast is still at work, and still points us to the feast prepared for all humankind.

> *You are not in the world for yourself.*
> *You have been sent here for others.*
> *The world is waiting for you.*
> Catherine Booth[91]

---

91   (1829–1890), co-founder of the Salvation Army with her husband William.

Bibliography

Citations in this book from French publications are the work of the author.

Blocher-Saillens, Madeleine. *Les Sept Paroles de la Croix*. Paris: Editions des Bons Semeurs, n.d.

Carmichael, Amy. *If*. Fort Washington, MD: CLC, 1938.

Chenu, Bruno; Prud'homme, Claude; Quéré, France; and Thomas, Jean-Claude. *The Book of Christian Martyrs*. London: SCM, 1990.

Clements, E. Anne. *Mothers on the Margin? The Significance of the Women in Matthew's Genealogy*. Eugene, OR: Pickwick, 2014.

De Boer, Esther, trans. Bowden, John. *Mary Magdalene*. London: SCM, 1997.

Delbrêl, Madeleine. *La Sainteté des Gens Ordinaires*, Œuvres complètes, Tome VII. Bruyères-le-Châtel: Nouvelle Cité, 2014.

Elliot, Elisabeth. *A Chance to Die: The Life and Legacy of Amy Carmichael*. Grand Rapids, MI: Revell, 1987.

Ellsberg, Robert. *Blessed Among All Women*. London: DLT, 2006.

Freeman, Curtis W., McClendon Jr., James Wm., Ewell, C. Rosalee Velloso. *Baptist Roots: A Reader in the Theology of a Christian People*. Valley Forge, PA: Judson Press, 1999.

Gilbert, Olive and Truth, Sojourner. *Narrative of Sojourner Truth*. Amazon, Great Britain, n.d.

Murray, Iain H. *Amy Carmichael 'Beauty for Ashes'*. Edinburgh: Banner of Truth Trust, 2015.

Montoya, Angéline. 'la famille Domon témoigne sur la disparition de Sœur Alice en Argentine'. https://www.la-croix.com/Actualite/Monde/La-famille-Domon-temoigne-sur-la-disparition-de-Soeur-Alice-en-Argentine-_NG_-2010-04-18-550124

Osiek, Carolyn and Balch, David. *Families in the New Testament World: Households and House Churches*. Louisville, KY: Westminster John Knox, 1997.

Pierron, Yvonne. *Missionnaire sous la dictature*. Paris: Editions du Seuil, 2007.

Pitaud, Bernard. *Prier 15 Jours avec Madeleine Delbrêl*. Bruyeres-le-Chatel: Nouvelle Cité, 1998.

Skobtsov, Mère Marie. *Le Sacrement du Frère*. Pully, Lausanne: Le Sel de la Terre, 1995.

Strom, Linda. *Karla Faye Tucker Set Free*. Colorado Springs, CO: Waterbrook, 2000.

ten Boom, Corrie, and Sherrill, John and Elizabeth. *The Hiding Place*. London: Hodder & Stoughton, 1971.

Viñoles, Diana Beatriz. *Lettres d'Alice Domon: Une disparue d'Argentine*. Paris: Karthala, 2016.

Whalin, Terry W. *Sojourner Truth: American Abolitionist*. Uhrichsville, OH: Barbour, 1997.

About the Author

Mary Cotes has been a regular contributor for many years to the quarterly *Preacher* magazine, and her sermons feature in the current *Canterbury Preacher's Companion 2020*, and in the forthcoming collection of the same title for 2021. Her devotional and liturgical material has appeared in numerous publications, not least in the collection of worship material written by women, *Gathering Up the Crumbs*, BUGB 2020. Writing also in French, she is the author of *Quand les femmes se mettent à l'oeuvre*, FAREL Excelsis, 2017, a contributor to *Ce que j'aimerais te confier*, FAREL Excelsis 2020, and a member of the editorial team of the website *ServirEnsemble*. She is also a qualified classical musician and teacher. She is married to Duncan and lives in Britain.

Photo credits: Marcus Armstrong

Publications

'Standing in the Stable,' in *Silence in Heaven: A Book of Women's Preaching*, ed. Heather Walton and Susan Durber, SCM Press, London, 1994.
Living Prayers for Today, compiler Maureen Edwards, IBRA, 1996.
Gathering for Worship, ed. Christopher J. Ellis and Myra Blyth, Canterbury Press, Norwich, 2005.

Prayers of the People, South Wales Baptist College, Cardiff and Regent's Park College, Oxford, 2011.
Gathering Up the Crumbs, BUGB, Didcot, 2020.
The Canterbury Preacher's Companion, Canterbury Press, Norwich, 2020, 2021 and 2022.

Books
Women Without Walls is the author's translation and revision of a book which she first wrote in French:
Quand les femmes se mettent à l'œuvre : les valeurs libératrices du Royaume des cieux, Farel, 2017. It is available at:
  https://www.clcfrance.com/quand-les-femmes-se-mettent-a-l-oeuvre_ref_FARQ130.html

The books are required reading for the bilingual 2021–23 leadership training programme of the Lifesprings School of Ministry/Formation Zoé, based in Lyon, France. For more information see https://lifesprings.org/formation-zoe/

www.ingramcontent.com/pod-product-compliance
Lightning Source LLC
LaVergne TN
LVHW041913070526
838199LV00051BA/2599